DATE DUE			
May 21 '74			
Jun18 '75			

THE FOSSIL EVIDENCE
FOR HUMAN
EVOLUTION

THE SCIENTIST'S LIBRARY

Biology and Medicine

EDITED BY

PETER P. H. De BRUYN, M.D.

THE FOSSIL EVIDENCE
FOR HUMAN
EVOLUTION

AN INTRODUCTION TO THE STUDY OF
PALEOANTHROPOLOGY

SECOND EDITION
REVISED AND ENLARGED

W. E. Le GROS CLARK

THE UNIVERSITY OF CHICAGO PRESS

CHICAGO & LONDON

International Standard Book Number: 0-226-10934-8 (clothbound)
Library of Congress Catalog Card Number: 64-22250

THE UNIVERSITY OF CHICAGO PRESS, CHICAGO 60637
The University of Chicago Press, Ltd., London

Preface to the Series

During the past few decades the investigative approaches to biological problems have become markedly diversified. This diversification has been caused in part by the introduction of methods from other fields, such as mathematics, physics, and chemistry, and in part has been brought about by the formulation of new problems within biology. At the same time, the quantity of scientific production and publication has increased. Under these circumstances, the biologist has to focus his attention more and more exclusively on his own field of interest. This specialization, effective as it is in the pursuit of individual problems, requiring ability and knowledge didactically unrelated to biology, is detrimental to a broad understanding of the current aspects of biology as a whole, without which conceptual progress is difficult.

The purpose of "The Scientist's Library: Biology and Medicine" series is to provide authoritative information about the growth and status of various subjects in such a fashion that the individual books may be read with profit not only by the specialist but also by those whose interests lie in other fields. The topics for the series have been selected as representative of active fields of science, especially those that have developed markedly in recent years as the result of new methods and new discoveries.

The textual approach is somewhat different from that ordinarily used by the specialist. The authors have been asked to emphasize introductory concepts and problems, and the present status of their subjects, and to clarify terminology and methods of approach instead of limiting themselves to detailed accounts of current factual knowledge. The authors have also been asked to assume a common level of scientific competence rather than to attempt popularization of the subject matter.

Consequently, the books should be of interest and value to

workers in the various fields of biology and medicine. For the teacher and investigator, and for students entering specialized areas, they will provide familiarity with the aims, achievements, and present status of these fields.

PETER P. H. DE BRUYN

CHICAGO, ILLINOIS

Preface

It seems desirable that this book should be prefaced by some explanation of its purpose. It is not intended, of course, to provide an account of all the fossil evidence bearing on hominid evolution, or even the greater part of it. It aims only to present some of the main sources of evidence in an abbreviated form and to indicate such conclusions as may justifiably be drawn from them. But it is concerned even more to examine critically the logical basis of the arguments and inferences which from time to time have been advanced on the basis of studies of the fossil material or of studies of the comparative anatomy of man and his nearest living relatives. Not so many years ago, fossil remains of hominids and anthropoid apes were very scanty; indeed, to those paleontologists who deal with vertebrate groups richly represented in the fossil record they must have appeared almost ridiculously so. In recent years they have been accumulating to a remarkable extent, and because of their importance in the elucidation of the origin of our own species, they naturally have a most compelling and personal interest. It is the more necessary, therefore, that their significance should be assessed objectively in accordance with the well-established principles of paleontological science. Paleoanthropologists are now becoming more critical in their appraisal of the available fossil evidence, and it is well that this should be so, for it is important, in considering the possible significance of new discoveries, to avoid some of the confusions and misunderstandings which have too often characterized discussions on human evolution in the past. Many of these misunderstandings have a terminological origin, and it has become more and more clear that they can be avoided in the future only if paleoanthropologists agree to the use of a common taxonomic nomenclature based on adequate definitions.

With the rapid accumulation of the fossil record of the Hominidae, much of the new material lately discovered has still to be described and compared in full detail. With such considerations in mind, it is quite apparent that some of the conclusions based on this paleontological evidence must necessarily be of a provisional nature. But it is right and proper to attempt an assessment of the available evidence from time to time, even if conclusions can be no more than provisional, for only by so doing is it possible to formulate working hypotheses which may be put to the test as more data come to hand.

Phylogenetic interpretations based on a fossil record which is still far from complete are, of course, meant to be no more than interpretations. They are offered for confirmation or modification as the record becomes more and more complete. Thus it is not claimed that the conclusions presented in this book are in any sense final. On the other hand, it is suggested that at least they accord reasonably well with the facts so far as these are at present available. And the facts which have in recent years become available now constitute a sequential record which, though by no means complete, does provide a substantial documentation of hominid evolution.

W. E. LE GROS CLARK

OXFORD

Table of Contents

Table of Contents

List of Figures

List of Figures

Morphological and Phylogenetic Problems of Taxonomy in Relation to Hominid Evolution

It is well recognized by comparative anatomists that there is a biological relationship between man and the anthropoid apes, in the sense that, by a process of gradual diversification, both have been derived in the distant past from a presumed common ancestral stock. When, in the early days of evolutionary studies, this inference was first made, it was based almost entirely on the totality of the anatomical resemblances between man and apes. Similar degrees of resemblance between other groups of mammals had been accepted as evidence of an evolutionary relationship; and in some cases this relationship had been further demonstrated and confirmed by the discovery of fossil remains of extinct creatures of intermediate type. But at the time of the publication of Darwin's book on the *Descent of Man* in 1871 the fossil record of human evolution was almost nonexistent, and the evidence for the relationship of man and apes—although it seemed convincing, even then, to many biologists—was only indirect. In more recent years, the fossil record bearing on human ancestry has accumulated to a remarkable extent. It is no longer meager in comparison with that of the evolution of some other mammalian groups, for it has provided much more direct and concrete evidence for the relationship of man and apes than was previously available. It is particularly noteworthy how closely some of these fossil types conform to intermediate stages of human evolution, which had been postulated and predicted on the basis of the indirect evidence of comparative anatomy. Discoveries of such fossil relics, indeed, provide a remarkable vindication of the well-

1

established methods of comparative morphology which have been used for the assessment of systematic affinities and phylogenetic relationships. As Watson (150) has noted, in arriving at a natural classification "individual animals . . . are allotted to their groups by structural similarities and differences, determined by observations directed by ordinary morphological reasoning. And the methods of morphology are shown to be valid because they enable us to make verifiable predictions." The progress of paleontological discovery has led to the verification of many of the predictions (based on the study of the comparative anatomy of Recent types) regarding the phylogenetic relationships and evolutionary origins of different groups of Primates. In this sense, indeed, paleontology might almost be called an experimental science, that is, if "experiment" is defined (as it is in the *Oxford Dictionary*) as "a procedure adopted for testing an hypothesis." Comparative anatomical studies of living forms may demonstrate a gradational series of morphological types, and such a series may suggest an actual temporal sequence of evolution. But the inference of a temporal sequence based on indirect evidence of this sort can be validated only by the direct evidence of paleontology.

1. COMPARATIVE ANATOMY AND TAXONOMY

Before considering the fossil evidence for the zoölogical relationship between man and ape, a brief reference may be made to the indirect evidence of anatomical resemblance. In spite of superficial appearances, these resemblances are actually very close. The bony skeleton, for example, is constructed on the same general plan; and in the case of some of its elements it may hardly be possible to make a clear distinction without a careful scrutiny of morphological details or the comparison of biometric data. It is precisely for this reason, of course, that quite sharp controversies in the past have occasionally been aroused over the identification of certain fossil fragments of a doubtful nature—whether they should be referred to ape or man. The muscular anatomy of man and apes is astonishingly alike, even down to some of the smaller details of attachments of many of the individual

2

muscles. The similarity in the structure and disposition of the visceral organs suggests that apes have a closer relationship to man than they have to the lower Primates. The human brain (though larger in relation to body size) in its morphology is little more than a magnified model of the brain of an anthropoid ape; indeed, there is no known element of the brain in the former which is not also to be found developed to some degree in the latter. All these facts, together with observations recording similar metabolic processes, serological reactions, chromosome patterns, blood groups, and so forth, are now well known. It is because of such a striking complex of resemblances that in schemes of zoölogical classification man and the anthropoid apes have for many years been placed quite close together, and in recent years the tendency has been for a still closer approximation.

Even the anti-evolutionary biologists of past days classified man in the Mammalia (they could hardly do otherwise), but they emphasized their conception of his apartness by placing him in a separate order, or even in a separate subclass, of mammals. More detailed and less subjective studies later placed him in the order Primates, according him a family status (Hominidae) which is equated with the Pongidae (anthropoid apes) and the Cercopithecidae (catarrhine monkeys). Today, the detailed morphological resemblances between man and the anthropoid apes are believed by many authorities to be more accurately expressed by grouping the Hominidae and Pongidae in a common superfamily, Hominoidea, and thus contrasting them both with the catarrhine monkeys—Cercopithecoidea (132). The closer association in a zoölogical classification of man and apes is no doubt due partly to the stricter application of taxonomic criteria, particularly as the result of the work of those authorities who are specially qualified by practical experience to apply the principles of vertebrate taxonomy to the Primates. But it is also due to the discovery of the fossil remains of primitive hominids in which the morphological distinctions contrasting *Homo sapiens* with the Recent anthropoid apes are not nearly so obtrusive.

Notwithstanding the numerous anatomical resemblances between Recent man and Recent apes, there are, of course, quite pronounced differences, and in the past these have all been duly emphasized by one anatomist or another. In some cases they have certainly been overemphasized, partly (it seems) because the human anatomist tends by the nature of his studies to focus attention on the minutiae of morphology and is thus inclined to exaggerate their taxonomic significance. Perhaps, also, the very personal nature of the problem has led some authorities to lay more stress on differences between man and apes than they would do on equivalent differences in other mammalian groups. The lists of morphological characters which from time to time have been put forward as evidence of man's "uniqueness" among mammals often give the strong impression that the authors were straining the evidence to the utmost limit (and sometimes a considerable way beyond it) in order to substantiate their thesis. It does not always seem to be fully realized that some of the unique features of *H. sapiens* on which the authors laid stress are merely distinctions at a generic or specific level, or that they represent little more than an extension of morphological trends which are quite apparent in other Primates. Nor was adequate account taken of the fact that similar claims for uniqueness might be equally valid for many other mammalian species. The giraffe, for example, possesses a number of anatomical characters which establish it as "unique" among all other living mammals, but its taxonomic position in the Giraffidae (equated with related families of the same infra-order, Pecora, such as the Cervidae and Bovidae) is accepted as a reasonable interpretation of its evolutionary status. Anatomically, *H. sapiens* is unique among mammals only in the sense that every mammalian species is in some features unique among mammals.

It is instructive to consider a sample of those anatomical differences which have been claimed to be so exclusively distinctive of the Hominidae as to demand an unusual degree of taxonomic isolation, and to see how these equate with differences found among other mammals which are accepted as forming natural groups in the phylogenetic sense. In *Homo* the large size of the brain relative to the body weight is certainly a feature which distinguishes this genus from all other Hominoidea, but it actually represents no more than an extension of the trend toward a progressive elaboration of the brain shown in the evolution of related Primates (and also of many other groups of eutherian mammals). In its morphological pattern, indeed, the human brain shows much less contrast with that of the large anthropoid apes than is found among the various families of an equivalent taxonomic category of Primates, the superfamily Lemuroidea; and even in its absolute size it shows less contrast than is to be found between the primitive and advanced genera of the single family Equidae. Several patterns of articulation between the bones of the skull have been claimed as quite distinctive of the Hominidae, but they also occur as variants (in some instances quite commonly) in the skulls of apes. In any case, however, the differences in pattern of articulation which are claimed to distinguish the Hominidae from the Pongidae are no more pronounced than those which are found to occur between different groups of (say) the single family Cercopithecidae. The dentition of the Hominoidea, in spite of differences between the Hominidae and Pongidae such as those of the relative size and shape of the canines and first lower premolars, actually shows far closer similarities than are to be found in the several families of (for example) the Feloidea. The linear proportions of the limbs in *H. sapiens* show certain well-recognized differences from those of the Recent anthropoid apes, but again these differences are not more marked than they are in (say) the several families of the Muroidea. Even the form of the glans penis and the fact that the female is characterized by a permanent, well-developed "bosom" have been adduced as evidence of "man's" uniqueness among mammals. But these may be no more than specific characters of *H. sapiens* and not characteristic features of the Hominidae as a whole (for, of course, we have no idea at all what the penis and the female breast may have been like in extinct types of man such as *Homo erectus*). These examples (which could well be multiplied) appear to indicate that anatomists who have laid such stress on differences of this sort as emphasizing the morphological "uniqueness" of *H. sapiens* have perhaps introduced a

5

personal and subjective element into their assessment of the taxonomic status of their own species.

2. MAN, *Homo sapiens,* AND THE HOMINIDAE

In order to eliminate the subjective factor as far as possible in discussions on hominid evolution, it seems quite essential to avoid colloquial terms such as "man" and "human." In recent controversies on the taxonomic position of fossil hominids, as so frequently in the past, their too common use has been a very obvious source of confusion. The fact is that these terms may not properly be used as though they were equivalent to the zoölogical terms *Homo* and Hominidae or to the adjectival form "hominid," in the same way that (for example) the term "horse" can be substituted for "equid." In the latter case, although the primitive equid *Hyracotherium* is so markedly different superficially from the modern *Equus,* it can be called a "primitive horse" without real danger of misunderstanding, for the term "horse" (or "horse family") still remains elastic enough in the minds of most people to permit its extension to relatively remote ancestral forms. Similarly, the fossil Hominoidea of Miocene age may appropriately be called "primitive anthropoid apes," even though they had not acquired all the specialized features which are accepted as characteristic of the anthropoid apes of today (see p. 186). But the terms "man" and "human" have come to assume, by common usage, a much narrower and more rigid connotation, which for most of us (however we may try to persuade ourselves otherwise) also involves a real emotional element. There can be little doubt that if these colloquial terms were to be rigidly excluded in strictly scientific discussions of the evolutionary origin of *H. sapiens,* and only the terms proper to taxonomy employed, such problems could be approached on a much more objective plane than often appears to be the case. The confusion to which the loose use of the term "man" may give rise is well illustrated by those comparative studies in which the skeletal elements of a fossil hominoid are compared with only the Recent anthropoid apes and with only *H. sapiens* (or perhaps even with only one or two racial varieties of *H. sapiens*) and the conclusion

6

is then drawn that in certain features the fossil agrees more close-ly with the "anthropoid apes" than with "man." The fallacy of such a statement is obvious, but it may nevertheless be very misleading to the casual reader. Clearly, the authors of such studies are using the term "man" as though it were equivalent to *H. sapiens,* or perhaps only one racial variety of *H. sapiens.* But the term "man" must presumably be taken also to include extinct types, such as Neanderthal man and the various representatives of *H. erectus.* These should be taken into consideration and also, of course, the extinct types of anthropoid ape. The fallacy of extrapolating from single species or genera to larger taxonomic groups is not uncommon in the literature of paleoanthropology.

Homo sapiens is one of the terminal products of an evolution-ary radiation that also led to the development of other types which have now become extinct, all of which are included in a natural group, the family Hominidae. If this familial term is to be used as it is in the definition of equivalent mammalian groups (i.e., with due reference to the fundamental concepts of evolution and to the taxonomic designation of other equivalent radiations), it must include not only *H. sapiens* but all those representatives of the evolutionary sequence which finally led to the development of this species (and of collateral lines) from the time when the sequence first became segregated from the evolutionary sequence of the Pongidae. Similarly, the family Pongidae logically includes not only the Recent anthropoid apes (gorilla, chimpanzee, orang, and gibbon) but also the fossil and extinct related types to which this particular line of evolutionary development gave rise after it had become clearly segregated from the common ancestral stock which also gave rise to the Cercopithecidae. It is of the utmost importance that those taking part in discussions on phylo-genetic sequences and zoölogical classification should recognize the implications of these taxonomic terms and make proper use of them. So far as the Hominoidea are concerned, they are illus-trated diagrammatically in Figure 1. From this diagram it will be seen that (as will be discussed in later chapters) two genera of the Hominidae are here provisionally recognized: *Homo*—repre-sented by the three species *H. sapiens, H. neanderthalensis,* and

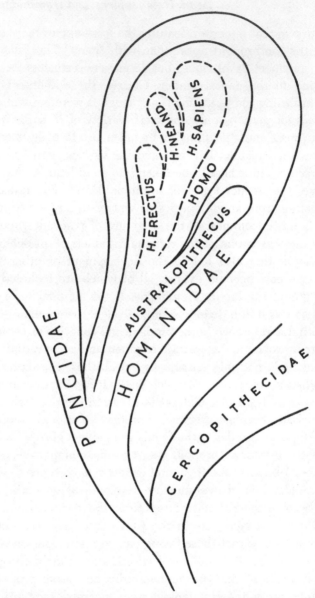

Fig. 1.—Diagram illustrating the probable phylogenetic relationship of the known genera of the Hominidae, and the relationship of the latter to the Pongidae. This diagram is also intended to emphasize that, as paleontological records in general clearly establish, representatives of an earlier genus may survive and persist long after other representatives of the *same* genus have given rise to a later genus. In other words, an ancestral genus may for some time actually be contemporary with its derivative genus.

H. erectus (an extinct type, previously regarded as a separate genus *Pithecanthropus*, which existed in the Far East and Africa during Early and Middle Pleistocene times) and *Australopithecus* —a primitive hominid whose fossilized remains have been recovered in great quantity from travertine deposits in South Africa and, more recently, from stratified deposits of the Olduvai gorge in Tanganyika. It still remains a matter of argument whether *Australopithecus* is represented by more than one species, or even whether it should be split into two or more genera. The phylogenetic relationships of hominid genera to one another and to the anthropoid ape family (Pongidae) indicated in the diagram are to be regarded as provisional interpretations based on the fossil evidence so far available. But the main intention of the diagram here is to make it clear that the Hominidae include all those genera and species which represent the earlier and later developments of a single evolutionary radiation, the latter being distinguished from the other radiation of the Hominoidea—the Pongidae—by a clear divergence of evolutionary trends. Similarly, the genus *Homo* or *Australopithecus* includes those species which represent in each case a common line of evolutionary development diverging from other species of the Hominidae. In other words, these terms are taken to connote a "vertical" classification of the Hominoidea, in the sense that they are indicative of separate main and subsidiary evolutionary sequences, ascending and diversifying from common basal stocks.[1] It is particularly urged that this simple and now generally accepted scheme of classification of the Hominoidea should be adhered to and that fancy terms invented from time to time by individual authors (such as Euhominids, Prehominids, Prehominians, Archanthropinae, Presapiens, and so forth) should be strenuously avoided. In so

[1] It is to be observed that mammalian classifications are not entirely of the "vertical" type. Where the fossil evidence is still wanting and in some cases where it is a matter of greater taxonomic convenience, terminal products of different lines of phylogenetic development may be grouped together in a "horizontal" type of classification. For example, in the Primates the Old World monkeys and the New World monkeys are at present grouped in a common suborder, the Anthropoidea, although there is sound evidence that these two groups of monkeys had their evolutionary origin in different groups of Eocene prosimians.

9

far as none of these terms has ever been properly defined, they remain entirely obscure, and, in so far as they remain obscure, their continued use is bound to lead to confusion.

One of the most important desiderata of a workable classification is that it should meet with a general (even if only provisional) adoption for common usage. Taxonomic systems usually involve a compromise of vertical and horizontal classifications, the former coming to predominate more and more as the fossil evidence of phylogenetic lines gradually accumulates; while this evidence remains incomplete, no two students of a particular mammalian group are likely to agree on all points of their classification. But they can, and should, agree to use a common system even if they do not accept all its implications, provided that the system represents at least a reasonable approximation to probable phylogenetic relationships and that it is broadly conceived in its basic plan. In the present work we make use of Simpson's classification of the Primates (132), not because it is the only possible classification, or on the assumption that it represents the last word on phylogenetic relationships (which no system of classification can do until the fossil record approximates to a complete record). We use it because (1) it is based on recognized authority and experience, (2) it has the merit of simplicity, (3) it appears to reflect reasonably closely such phylogenetic relationships as can be inferred from the evidence at hand (and as far as this can be done in any system of classification without seriously affecting convenience of reference), and (4) it has been provisionally accepted and recognized by other authoritative workers in the same field. It is well to emphasize this last consideration, for only by the provisional acceptance of a common scheme of classification (with common and well-understood taxonomic terms) is it possible for zoölogists or anthropologists to engage in mutual discussions on problems of Primate evolution without misunderstandings and misrepresentations.

One of the most remarkable sources of confusion in recent discussions on hominid evolution is the tacit assumption by some writers that a large brain is an essential character of the Hominidae; this example is referred to here because it serves to illustrate rather forcibly the misuse of taxonomic terms. Now it is, of course, obvious that one of the outstanding characteristics of *H. sapiens* is the relatively large size of the brain. But some of those anatomists who lay most stress on this distinction also maintain that the Hominidae (i.e., the family comprising the evolutionary radiation leading, *inter alia*, to *H. sapiens*) separated from the other radiations of the Primates at a very remote geological period—at least by the Early Miocene. On the other hand (as we shall later see), there is no evidence to show that the precursors of *H. sapiens* acquired a brain size approaching modern dimensions before the Early Pleistocene and certainly not before the Upper Pliocene. Consequently, there must presumably have been a very lengthy period in the hominid sequence of evolution during which the brain still retained a size approximating to that of the modern large apes. In other words, while a large brain may be accepted as one of the diagnostic characters of the species *H. sapiens*, it is not a valid criterion of the family Hominidae. In a well reasoned essay it has been suggested by Oakley (102), that the term "man" (and presumably "human" as well) should be reserved for those later representatives of the hominid sequence of evolution who had reached a level of intelligence indicated by their capacity to fabricate implements of some sort. Man, that is to say, is essentially a tool-making creature. If this definition is accepted, then the earlier small-brained representatives of the Hominidae who had not yet developed this capacity may conveniently be referred to "the prehuman phase of hominid evolution."

The assumption that a brain of large dimensions is a distinctive feature of the Hominidae as contrasted with the Pongidae is certainly in part the result of a terminological confusion resulting from the loose usage of the terms "man" and "human" as though they were equivalent to "hominid." But it has also been argued (again mainly on the basis of comparative anatomical studies of living forms) that the primary factor which led to the evolutionary divergence of the Hominidae from the Pongidae was the rapid enlargement of the brain and that other distinctive characters, such as those related to posture and gait, were secondary developments. However, apart from the fact that functional considerations make such a speculative hypothesis unlikely or, indeed, impossible, it is rendered untenable by the paleontological data now available.

It has been necessary to divaricate on the significance of the taxonomic terms used in discussions on hominid evolution, for the reason that much fruitless argument has evidently been expended for the want of careful definitions, and it may be well to reemphasize briefly one or two of the major points discussed. The purpose of zoölogical classification, as Simpson has pointed out, is primarily a matter of practical convenience; but the basis of a taxonomic system is phylogenetic, and the criteria of the definition of taxonomic terms should, as far as is consistent with practical convenience, be consonant with the evidence of phylogeny. It is for this reason, of course, that zoölogical classifications must necessarily be provisional and tentative in the absence of a substantial paleontological record, and they need constant revision as this record becomes more and more complete. In the absence of any fossil remains, the family Equidae would presumably be defined (as Cuvier, indeed, defined his equivalent of this family) on the basis of the existing species of *Equus*—that is to say, by characters such as the single complete digit on each foot and the complicated pattern of the cheek teeth. But, with the accession of fossil material, the definition of Equidae has come to be widely extended to include such primitive representatives of the equid sequence of evolution as *Hyracotherium* and *Mesohippus*. In defining the Hominidae and contrasting this family with the Pongidae, considerations of phylogeny must also be taken into account. In other words, a satisfactory definition is to be obtained only by a consideration of the fundamental factors of structural evolution which determined the initial segregation of the Hominidae and the Pongidae from a common ancestral stock, and of the divergent trends which the two evolutionary sequences followed in their later development. The former consideration is no doubt of more direct importance in the identification of fossil remains of early hominoids whose taxonomic status may not be immediately clear, for in such primitive types some of the later evolutionary trends will not yet have manifested themselves to any marked degree. Those anatomical features which probably have no more than a specific value for the definition of *H. sapiens* (such as the combination of a large brain with a vertical forehead, small teeth, reduced jaws, presence of a chin, and so forth) must obviously be avoided in the definition of the Hominidae.

While in any system of classification the lower taxonomic categories, such as genera and species, may be defined in more or less static terms (at least in so far as they concern divergent rather than successional types), it is impracticable to draw up any comprehensive definition of larger categories, such as families and orders, except on the basis of evolutionary trends. The latter may be inferred indirectly by a consideration of the various end-products of evolution in each group, but they can be ultimately demonstrated only by paleontological sequences. For example, the order Primates is particularly difficult to define by reference to fixed characters, mainly for the reason that, as a group, it is not distinguished by any gross forms of adaptive specialization possessed by all its members in common. The evolutionary progress of the Primates, as Simpson (133) has well said, has been in the direction of greater adaptability rather than of greater adaptation. Thus the order can be defined only by reference to the prevailing evolutionary trends which have distinguished it from other groups—such as the progressive development of large and complicated brains, the elaboration of the visual apparatus and a corresponding reduction of the olfactory apparatus, the abbreviation of the facial skeleton, the tendency toward the elimination of the third incisor tooth and of one or two premolars, the preservation of a relatively simple pattern of the molar teeth, the replacement of sharp claws (falculae) by flattened nails (ungulae), the retention of pentadactyl limbs with an accentuation of the mobility of the digits, and so forth (84). Not all Primates (even those that exist today) have developed all these characters or completed their development to the same degree. And still less so, of course, was this the case with the earliest Primates of the Eocene period.

3. The Early Differentiation of the
Hominidae and Pongidae

As we have already noted, the expansion of the brain to the large dimensions characteristic of *H. sapiens* was evidently a relatively late phenomenon in the sequence of hominid evolution. What, then, are the basically distinctive characters whose development initiated the evolutionary radiation of the Hominidae in the first stages of its segregation from the Pongidae and which might therefore be expected to be of importance for the differentiation of the *earlier* representatives of these two families? From a consideration of the details of comparative anatomy of living forms and from the evidence now available from fossil hominoids, it appears reasonably certain (and, indeed, is agreed by authorities who hold widely differing views on a number of phylogenetic details) that the most important single factor in the evolutionary emergence of the Hominidae as a separate and independent line of development was related to the specialized functions of erect bipedal locomotion (148). Herein the Hominidae showed a most marked evolutionary divergence from the Pongidae, for in the latter the strongly contrasting brachiating mode of locomotion was developed. In the one case the lower limb increased in length in relation to the trunk length and to the length of the upper limb; in the other it was the upper limb that increased in relative length. In other words, in the relative growth of the limbs the Pongidae and the Hominidae have followed two opposing allometric trends. In the Hominidae the bony elements of the foot and the knee joint became modified in shape and proportions to permit the structural stability required for bipedal progression; in the Pongidae the mobility of these parts was enhanced for specialized prehensile functions. In the Hominidae the pelvic skeleton underwent quite far-reaching changes directly related to the erect posture; in the Pongidae it retained the general shape and proportions found in lower Primates generally. These divergent modifications of the limbs and pelvis are related to very different modes of life in the two families. They involve more than just those proportional differ-

14

ences in linear dimensions which can be determined by over-all measurements and about which so much detailed and accurate information has been accumulated by the patient studies of Schultz (119, 121, 123), for they are also accompanied by quite marked structural divergences in muscular anatomy (as Straus, 140, has emphasized). The total morphological pattern of the limbs and pelvis in the known representatives of the Hominidae thus presents a criterion by which these are distinguished rather abruptly from the known representatives of the Pongidae. If, as now appears probable, this distinction was the factor responsible for the primary segregation of these two evolutionary radiations, it provides a most important clue for assessing the true taxonomic position of their early representatives.

Another criterion of special importance in paleontology is provided by the total morphological pattern of the dentition. In all the Recent Pongidae the primitive features of the Primate dentition have been modified by the widening of the incisor series, the replacement of a forwardly converging molar-premolar series by parallel (or slightly divergent) tooth rows, the accentuation of powerful overlapping canines (with a pronounced sexual dimorphism), and the development of a more strongly sectorial character of the anterior lower premolar. It may be noted here that a sectorial type of lower premolar, which is characteristic of all Recent anthropoid apes, is a predominantly unicuspid tooth, the main cusp having anteriorly a cutting edge which shears against the upper canine (see Fig. 26, *B, 1*). In all the known Hominidae the incisors remain small, the molar-premolar series converge anteriorly in a rounded arcade, the canines have undergone a relative reduction in size and do not overlap to any marked degree (and not at all after the early stages of attrition, except in some individuals of the Pleistocene genus, *Homo erectus*), and the anterior lower premolar is of a bicuspid, nonsectorial form. These differences in the dentition may have been secondary to those of the limbs and pelvis, but the paleontological evidence indicates that they also became manifested relatively early in the evolutionary history of the two families.

15

4. Total Morphological Pattern

Reference has been made earlier to the "total morphological pattern" presented by limb structure or the dentition. It seems desirable to stress this concept of pattern rather strongly because the assessment of the phylogenetic and taxonomic status of fossil hominoid remains must be based, not on the comparison of individual characters in isolation one by one, but on a consideration of the *total pattern* which they present in combination. Vertebrate taxonomists are, of course, well accustomed to taking account of groups of characters in their assessments of the zoölogical status of an animal, and they are quite conversant with the phrase "character complex." But anthropologists and human anatomists (perhaps from lack of experience in the practice and principles of taxonomy) often tend to focus their attention rather on single characters in their discussion of relationships; or, if they take into account a list of several characters, they tend to treat them as an assemblage of separate individual units, without recognizing that in combination they constitute a functional pattern which must be treated as a whole. It is in order to emphasize this most important principle that the term "pattern" is put forward as somewhat equivalent to (but actually meaning more than) the term "complex." Undoubtedly, many of the conflicting opinions expressed in the past by comparative anatomists regarding the relationships of the Hominidae and other Primates have been the result of the separate comparison of *individual* characters. In fact, however, it is doubtful whether any single structural detail or measurement by itself can be accepted as providing a clear-cut distinction which would permit a positive identification of a single specimen of a fossil hominoid. For example, the mere presence of a measurable gap (diastema) between the upper canine and lateral incisor teeth is not by itself sufficient to determine that a fragment of a fossil hominoid jaw is identifiable as that of an anthropoid ape rather than a hominid (though a diastema is very rarely absent in the completely erupted dentition of anthropoid apes and is very rarely found in a hominid jaw). But if a well-marked diastema forms one element of a complicated morphological pattern which also includes conical, projecting, and overlapping canine teeth, a laterally compressed lower first premolar tooth of sectorial form, forwardly placed incisors, and so forth, it becomes an important feature in the taxonomic identification of a fossil specimen, for such a pattern is diagnostic of the Pongidae in contradistinction to the Hominidae. Or, to take another example, the mere presence in one specimen of a primitive type of skull of a "mastoid process," considered simply and solely as a bony eminence, does not by itself identify it as hominid rather than pongid, for a mastoid process *of a sort* may occasionally be found in the skulls of mature gorillas (as Schultz, 122, has noted). But if a mastoid process of typical hominid shape, disposition, and proportions is found *consistently* in a number of skulls in a common collection of fossil hominoids (immature as well as mature) and if it also forms a component part of a total morphological pattern of associated parts normally found in hominid, but never in pongid, skulls (including a clear-cut digastric fossa and a well-marked occipital groove, and a characteristic relationship to the nuchal area of the occipital bone and to a tympanic plate of a particular conformation), its significance for taxonomic purposes evidently becomes enormously enhanced. Many similar examples could be adduced (and some will later be noted) of a coincidence of total morphological pattern which has been overlooked or obscured by treating in isolation only one or two features of the pattern and assuming that these are by themselves adequate for the assessment of taxonomic affinities.

5. Convergent and Parallel Evolution

It is a fundamental principle of taxonomy that a closeness of resemblance in total morphological pattern is an indication of a corresponding closeness in zoölogical relationship. On the other hand, it is also generally recognized that structural resemblances of a sort can be produced by convergent and parallel evolution, and in this case they are not of equal value in the assessment of relationships. Taxonomists are well aware of these complica-

tions and of the need to take account of them. But the potentialities of convergence and parallelism have been much over-
estimated by some comparative anatomists, who have sought
to discount the structural resemblances between *H. sapiens*
and the anthropoid apes by attributing most (if not all) of them
to these processes. That some degree of convergent and parallel
evolution has occurred in the Hominidae and Pongidae is not
in doubt; but to attribute all those similarities which form
component elements of a highly complicated total morphological
pattern to long-standing convergence or parallelism reduces the
morphological principles underlying taxonomy to an absurdity.
By the skilful manipulation of such extreme misapplications of
well-known evolutionary processes (and, incidentally, taking
no account of the statistical improbabilities at once made evident by a consideration of the principles of genetics), it is possible for anyone to draw those conclusions regarding systematic
affinities which conform most with his personal predilections.
There is no need here to enlarge on this matter of convergence
and parallelism in relation to taxonomy (or on the misconcep-
tions which some authorities have held on the degree to which
evolution is irreversible), for such questions have recently been
dealt with in a thoroughly reasonable manner by paleontologists well qualified to do so by long experience and recognized
distinction. But it is worth while quoting Simpson (134) that
"the basis of parallelism is initial similarity of structure and adaptive type, with subsequent recurrent homologous mutation"; that
the initial similarity and the homology of mutations themselves
imply phylogenetic relationship; that "closeness of parallelism
tends to be proportional to closeness of affinity"; and that "it is
improbable that convergence ever produces literal identity in
structure and certainly no such case has ever been demonstrated."
The extensive data of comparative anatomy and vertebrate paleontology now available justify the assumption (at any rate as a
reasonably secure working hypothesis) that species and genera
which show a preponderance of structural resemblances are genetically related forms, unless some flagrant discrepancy exists in
one or more features such as could be explained morphologically

18

only by a long period of independent evolution from an ancestral form of a much more primitive type (and not, as may, of course, occur, by mutational variations of a geologically more recent date). It may not always be possible to exclude finally the factor of convergence as an explanation of a similarity in individual structural features; but it is not permissible to dismiss a complicated pattern of morphological resemblances as merely the expression of convergence, without presenting evidence in support of such an arbitrary "explanation." As Colbert (29) has pointed out, "parallelism should not be invoked to explain resemblances among related animals unless it can be proved, for to do this is to make the whole concept of evolution largely meaningless."

6. THE MULTIPLICATION OF GENERA AND SPECIES

Among the more vexing taxonomic problems of Primate paleontology is the somewhat arbitrary multiplication of genera and species on the basis of skeletal remains which in many cases are very fragmentary. This, of course, is also a problem of vertebrate paleontology in general. Skeletal elements by themselves do not always reflect to the same degree those differences which are apparent enough in the living animal to warrant distinction at a specific, or even a generic, level. For example, in the Recent Cercopithecoidea the comparative odontologist might not always find it easy to justify—on the basis of the dentition alone—some of the specific distinctions which are clearly justified by a study of the animals as a whole. On the other hand, these very examples may lead him to attribute an exaggerated importance to trivial details of the dentition in *other* groups of Primates in which they may be no more than an expression of individual (or subspecific) variation. Particularly is this the case with the study of fossil remains of the Hominoidea; for the individual, sexual, and subspecific variations in this group of Primates are rather considerable (see Remane, 109). There is thus an almost inevitable (and perhaps, therefore, excusable) tendency among Primate paleontologists too readily to multiply species or genera among the fossil remains which they study, if these are only few and fragmentary, for the obvious reason that the extent of the individual and group variability can hardly be assessed until a much more complete record becomes available. But this initial tendency toward "splitting," provided that it is recognized, is perhaps not of great importance; and it is often a matter of convenience to accept provisionally and temporarily the generic and specific differentiations which have been made by a paleontologist in the first instance, even though there may be some doubt about their taxonomic validity. Later on, as more fossil material becomes available or as the result of a more detailed comparative analysis of the relevant structural details, the initial taxonomic distinctions may need to be revised. The genus *Sinanthropus* ("Pekin man") was at first based on a single tooth, and the name was retained and employed for many years, even by those who felt dubious about its validity. With further discoveries in China and Java, it became clear that *Sinanthropus* was really not distinguishable generically from *Pithecanthropus* ("Java man"), and it was included in this genus of early hominids. Now, however, even the generic term *Pithecanthropus* has been discarded, for it has been agreed by most anthropologists that the type to which it was applied comes more properly within the genus *Homo*, with the specific distinction of *Homo erectus* (see p. 88). The Chinese representative of this extinct species may still be distinguished at the subspecific level from the Javanese representative, and it is a distinction which is convenient to retain, pending the accession of further material which may allow a more complete study of the limits of variance in the two groups. Another example illustrating the difficulties of taxonomy in the study of fossil remains is furnished by the discovery of *Australopithecus* in South Africa (see p. 127). The first skull to be found was described by Dart (33), who created for it the specific name *Australopithecus africanus*. Subsequently, Broom found many more remains of individuals belonging to the same group and thought that he was able to distinguish other genera and species—*Plesianthropus transvaalensis* (found at Sterkfontein), *Paranthropus robustus* (found at Kromdraai), *Paranthropus crassidens*, and *Telanthropus capensis* (both found at Swartkrans). More recently, a new generic term, *Zinjanthropus*, has been conferred on an australopithecine fossil found at Olduvai in Tanganyika. It is probably true to say that most authorities have now agreed that a convincing case has not yet been made out for separating these fossils generically (see p. 167). However, it may be in some cases a matter of convenience in preliminary discussions to refer to provisional taxonomic terms of this kind, though, of course, this does not commit those who do so to their final acceptance. On the other hand, where there is a large element of doubt, the wisest procedure (pro tem) is to use place-names referring to the site of discovery and to speak (for example) of the "Sterkfontein skull," of the "Kromdraai mandible," or of the "Swartkrans pelvis." In view of the conflicting opinions still held on the nomenclature of the fossil representatives of *Australopithecus,* they are commonly referred to collectively as the subfamily Australopithecinae, or, colloquially, the australopithecines.

It is a matter of great difficulty to formulate precisely the criteria by reference to which specific or generic distinctions are recognized in fossil material. Particularly is this so when the material is scanty and it is not possible to determine the limits of individual, sexual, and age variability. In such cases the paleontologist can only proceed on the assumption that these limits are of much the same order as in closely related groups where they are reasonably well known. For this purpose a sound knowledge of such related groups (as well as a considerable taxonomic experience) is obviously a prerequisite, for different skeletal and dental characters show different degrees of variation in different groups. Thus even considerable variation in the size of the molar teeth and jaws or in the cranial capacity in a group of fossil hominids should not delude the paleontologist into making specific distinctions on the basis of such characters alone, for the latter are known to show a very wide range of variation in the single species *H. sapiens.* On the other hand, similar degrees of variation found among the fossil remains of certain lower Primates may justify a specific distinction in so far as the same characters are known to be less variable in these types. On the basis of such analogies, it is legitimate to make specific or generic distinctions as a provisional taxonomic device (even when the

21

fossil material is scanty); but the validity of these distinctions can, of course, be finally determined only when sufficiently abundant material is available for comparative study.

The reaction in recent years against the tendency by paleo-anthropologists to multiply genera and species on the basis of minor and insignificant differences in very fragmentary specimens is a particularly welcome reaction and, as some may think, long overdue. It will certainly bring about a far-reaching revision of many generic and specific terms which in the past have been too hastily coined for fossil pongids and hominids. For example, if it is now agreed that the morphological differences between *"Pithecanthropus"* and modern man are not adequate to justify a generic distinction, and that the former type should be taxonomically denoted as *Homo erectus,* there can no longer be any possible excuse on morphological grounds for separating *"Paranthropus," "Zinjanthropus,"* and other australopithecines from the genus *Australopithecus.* They may, of course, represent different species of this genus, but in some cases even this degree of distinction seems doubtful.

In an illuminating essay, Dr. E. Simons (131) has referred to the claims occasionally made by those who have discovered fossil relics of early man in one region that it is in that particular locality that the evolutionary origin of man took place. The author first emphasizes that the over-splitting of fossil types of hominids and pongids by taxonomists has in large part been due to the tendency to regard geographical separation, and even moderate differences in geological age, as indicative of genetic incompatibility in spite of close morphological resemblances. But, as he points out, during the geological periods of the Miocene and Pliocene, that is, at a time when the Hominidae and Pongidae were undergoing a progressive diversification from a common ancestral stock, there were quite considerable faunal migrations to and fro between Asia, Europe, and Africa. Among other mammalian types these faunal interchanges included extinct anthropoid apes as well as possible forerunners of man, and they involved not only single genera but in some cases probably single species. It thus no longer makes sense to postulate that

22

"man" evolved in one particular and restricted geographical locality—such as in India or the Far East, or in Europe, or in North, East, or South Africa. The progenitors of the Hominidae and the earliest representatives of this family may well have been distributed as wide-spread interbreeding communities over several of these regions.

It seems sometimes to have been assumed (in referring to fossil specimens) that specific or generic distinctions are disallowed if intergradations between these taxonomic categories are demonstrable. However, such a criterion is clearly not applicable to a temporal sequence (nor, indeed, is it always so in a contemporary series of geographically or ecologically segregated groups). If a complete fossil record of the Hominidae were available, there would presumably be complete intergradations from the earliest to the latest representatives of this evolutionary sequence. This would not eliminate the need to make taxonomic distinctions in order to give expression to the various subsidiary radiations of the sequence, though naturally the distinctions become less and less obvious as the paleontological record leads back to the *initial* stages of evolutionary segregation of each radiation. Intergeneric gradations in a temporal sequence are well exemplified in the Equidae, for Simpson (135) remarks, in reference to *Hipparion* and related forms, that the difference from the ancestral type *Merychippus* "is clear-cut and, indeed, obvious when the most characteristic forms are compared, but the change was gradual and even an expert is puzzled as to where to draw the line in the continuous series from advanced *Merychippus* to primitive *Hipparion, Neohipparion,* or *Nannippus.*" On the other hand, the discovery of intergradations in the fossil record may be of some importance, in so far as they facilitate (or confirm) natural groupings in the major taxonomic categories, such as families, suborders, and orders, for they may betray systematic affinities which are not always fully apparent when the terminal products of phylogenetic lines are alone considered. For example, in the classification of the Primates a comparison of the living tarsier with the existing lemurs suggests a contrast so pronounced as to justify a subordinal distinction between tarsioids and lemuroids.

But a study of prosimians of Eocene date has demonstrated that, in their dentition and skull, these early Primates may present such a mixture of characters as to suggest that tarsioids and lemuroids have originated (independently of other groups of Primates) from a common ancestral stock. This inference finds expression in the inclusion in Simpson's classification of tarsioids and lemuroids in the same suborder, Prosimii; but their early evolutionary segregation is at the same time reflected in their taxonomic separation into different infra-orders. So far as the Hominoidea are concerned, the taxonomic association of the Hominidae and the Pongidae in a common superfamily, Hominoidea, depends partly (as already noted) on the discovery of fossil remains showing what appears to be a considerable degree of structural intergradation between the two families.

7. The Quantitative Assessment of Taxonomic Relationships

Apart from the problem of assessing general taxonomic relationships by reference to morphological resemblances so far as these may be determined by direct comparisons, attempts have from time to time been made to estimate degrees of resemblance (and thus, it is assumed, degrees of affinity) on a quantitative basis. This biometrical approach is an attempt to facilitate and place on a strictly objective basis the comparison of one type with another. But unfortunately it is fraught with the greatest difficulties, the main one of which, no doubt, is the impossibility by known methods of weighting each individual character according to its taxonomic relevance. If the measurements of every single morphological character of skull, dentition, and limb bones were of equal value for the assessment of zoölogical affinities, it might be practicable to assess the latter in strictly quantitative terms. But it is very well recognized that this is by no means the case. It is well known also that the products of convergent evolution may lead to similarities (particularly in general over-all measurements and indices derived therefrom) which, if expressed quantitatively, would give an entirely false idea of systematic proximity. Generally speaking, it is true to say that statistical comparisons of over-all measurements and indices are of the greatest value in assessing degrees of affinity in forms already known to be quite closely related—e.g., subspecies or geographical races—but they become of less and less practical value as the relationship becomes more remote and the types to be compared become more disparate. This was made clearly evident in the pioneer studies of Pearson and Bell (107) on the femur of the Primates. For while their comparisons of the dimensions and indices of the femur in Recent man (*H. sapiens*) and his Paleolithic precursors (e.g., *H. neanderthalensis* and *H. erectus*) clearly provide data of considerable value for assessing their relative affinities, the phylogenetic interpretations which they give to their comparisons with lower Primates not only are very meager and tentative in relation to the vast amount of work which their analysis has entailed but are not always in accord with the paleontological evidence which has since become available. But this is not to depreciate the importance of the studies of Pearson and Bell. If there are faults in their work, they are the faults of pioneers applying their technique to a field with which they were not thoroughly conversant, and, of course, their statistical methods have now in some cases been superseded by more reliable techniques. They specifically stated that their studies were to be regarded as experimental—to see how much could be ascertained (in regard to systematic affinities) by the intensive biometrical study of single bones. It will probably be agreed that the results of this experiment, relying on only a few indices based on over-all measurements and not taking into full account such factors as body size, were largely negative. But it will also be agreed that it was an experiment well worth trying.

Since the original studies of Pearson and his colleagues, the application of biometrics to taxonomic inquiries has become commonplace. But, because statistical methods are sometimes applied uncritically and without due appreciation of the morphological and phylogenetic basis of taxonomy or of the fundamentals of the phenomena underlying the data to be measured, they have been open to criticism and are in serious danger of becoming discredited. For this reason it seems worthwhile drawing attention to a number of fallacies which are often overlooked by workers in this field, particularly by anthropologists who are not morphologists by training or who are not statistical experts. They are listed here, not in any spirit of criticism, but in the earnest hope that, by their careful avoidance in the future, some common sources of confusion may be avoided in discussions on the evolutionary origin of man.

THE FALLACY OF RELYING ON INADEQUATE
STATISTICAL DATA

One of the limitations of the biometric analysis of taxonomic characters depends on the fact that, if adequate statistical methods are employed, the analysis of even a few measurements entails a very considerable amount of work. Consequently, there is a danger of relying on too few measurements, a danger which is, of course, very seriously increased if these happen to have little taxonomic relevance. The comparison of such measurements may lead to the statement that (say) a fossil bone or tooth shows no significant difference from that of *H. sapiens,* or perhaps from that of the Recent anthropoid apes. But, clearly, such a statement is of doubtful value (and may actually be very misleading) if at the same time account is not taken of other morphological features which may, in fact, be much more relevant for assessing affinities. An example of this difficulty is provided by the famous case of *Hesperopithecus.* This generic name was given to a fossil tooth found in Nebraska in 1922, on the assumption that it represented an extinct type of anthropoid ape. Part of the evidence for this assumption was based on a comparison of the over-all measurements of the tooth with a series of ape teeth, for these metrical data established clearly that in this respect the fossil tooth falls within the range of variation shown in Recent apes (47). However, it was the critical eye of a comparative anatomist, with a long experience of the examination and discrimination of paleontological material, which drew attention to certain "nonmetrical" morphological details throwing serious doubt on the original interpretation. As is well known, the tooth proved later to be that of a fossil peccary. This example, which has a certain historical interest in the field of Primate paleontology, is quoted here not in criticism of those who were responsible for the mistaken identification (there can be few paleontologists who have not erred in this way at some time or another!), but to emphasize that two or three over-all measurements of a tooth can express only an insignificant proportion of all those metrical elements which contribute to its shape as a whole. This applies also, of course, to skulls or individual bones.

THE FALLACY OF TREATING ALL METRICAL DATA AS OF EQUAL TAXONOMIC VALUE

It has already been emphasized that morphological characters vary greatly in their significance for the assessment of affinities. Consequently, it is of the utmost importance that, in applying statistical methods, particular attention should be given to those characters whose taxonomic relevance has been duly established by comparative anatomical and paleontological studies. This *principle of taxonomic relevance* in the selection of characters for biometrical comparisons is one of great importance, but it is also rather liable to be overlooked. It may be asked how the distinction is to be made between morphological characters which are relevant or irrelevant for taxonomic purposes. The answer to this question is that each natural group of animals is defined (on the basis of data mainly derived from comparative anatomy and paleontology) by a certain pattern of morphological characters which its members possess in common and which have been found by the pragmatic test of experience to be sufficiently distinctive and consistent to distinguish its members from those of other related groups. The possession of this common morphological pattern is taken to indicate a community of origin (in the evolutionary sense) of all the members of the group, an assumption of which the justification is to be found in the history of paleontological discovery. But, as a sort of fluctuating background to the common morphological pattern, there may be a number of characters, sometimes obviously adaptive, which not only vary widely within the group but overlap with similar variations in other groups. Such fluctuating characters may be of importance

27

for distinguishing (say) one species from another within the limits of the family, but they may be of no value by themselves for distinguishing this family from related families. In other words, they are taxonomically irrelevant so far as interfamilial relationships are concerned. The same applies to other major taxonomic categories such as superfamilies, subfamilies, and so forth. For example, among the lemurs the over-all dimensions (length and breadth) of the molar teeth may provide useful criteria for distinguishing between the various species and sub-species of the Galaginae or between those of the Lorisinae, but they could not be expected to be of any value in differentiating between these two subfamilies.

So far as the Hominidae are concerned, the principle of taxonomic relevance may be illustrated by reference to the extinct species *Homo erectus* (see p. 91). The available evidence indicates that in this type the morphological features of the skull and jaws are very different from those of *H. sapiens,* while the limb skeleton is hardly distinguishable. Clearly, therefore, if the question arises as to whether the remains of a fossil hominid are those of *H. erectus* or *H. sapiens,* for taxonomic purposes the morphological features of the skull and jaws are the relevant characters to which attention should be primarily directed. In the study of fossils representing early phases in evolutionary radiations, their affinities must be determined by a study of those characters whose taxonomic relevance may be inferred from a consideration of the main trends of evolution as demonstrated by comparative anatomical studies and by extrapolation from the fossil record, so far as the latter is available. For example, as we have already seen, the initial evolutionary segregation of the Hominidae from the Pongidae was almost certainly dependent on modifications related to the development of an erect bipedal gait (see Washburn, 148, on this point). Hence, in assessing the affinities of the *earlier* representatives of the Hominidae (whose taxonomic position may be in some doubt), the skeletal characters of the pelvis and hind limb are likely to be of much greater importance than those of the forelimb. As we shall see later, also, the morphological details of the dentition are likely to be of much greater taxonomic relevance than the actual over-all dimensions of the teeth and jaws or the cranial capacity. As a further example of the principle of taxonomic relevance, we may refer to the dentition of some of the fossil representatives of the Pongidae. In these the incisor teeth are so similar to those of *Homo* (and even *H. sapiens*) as hardly to be distinguishable. On the other hand, in all known pongids the canine teeth are quite different. Obviously, therefore, in determining as between the pongid or hominid affinities of a fossil hominoid, the canines have a much higher degree of taxonomic relevance than the incisors.

It perhaps needs to be emphasized that the principle of taxonomic relevance must also, of course, be taken into account in any attempt to assess the affinities of a fossil type from the biometrical study of a single skeletal element. For not all the dimensions or indices of such a specimen will have the same taxonomic relevance, and some may have none at all for the particular comparison under consideration. The pelvic bone of the fossil Australopithecinae from South Africa (see p. 157) provides a good example of this point, and it also illustrates the essential importance of distinguishing between those morphological characters which may be similar in two divergent evolutionary groups simply because they are inherited from a common ancestry and those characters which represent adaptive modifications peculiar to, and are thus distinctive and diagnostic of, either one or the other of the two groups. The former type of character is obviously not taxonomically relevant for distinguishing the two groups (at least in the earlier stages of their evolutionary development); the latter type evidently has a high degree of taxonomic relevance. The australopithecine pelvic bone presents a most interesting combination of characters. Some of these are quite distinctive of the hominid (as opposed to the pongid) line of evolution, such as the width-height ratio of the ilium, the development of a strong anterior inferior iliac spine, the orientation of the sacral articulation, the formation of a deep sciatic notch, and so forth; and together they comprise a morphological pattern which is evidently an adaptation to the mechanical requirements of an erect posture. On the other hand, there appear to be no characters which are definitely distinctive of the pongid (as opposed to the hominid) line of evolution. It is true that in certain features the pelvic bone is rather more primitive than that of modern man, and in these particular features it does show some degree of resemblance to that of the modern anthropoid apes. But such a resemblance is clearly due to the retention of primitive features derived from a common hominoid ancestry and is thus not indicative of any close affinity with the modern anthropoid apes; this is made quite clear by the fact (as we have just noted) that, in those features in which the australopithecine pelvis *has* undergone modification away from the primitive ancestral type, the modification has followed the direction of hominid evolution and not of pongid evolution. It is these latter (positive) features, therefore, which are relevant for determining the taxonomic status of the Australopithecinae so far as the pelvic bone is concerned.

In order to keep within reasonable limits the number of measurements to be used for the statistical comparison of a fossil bone or tooth with related types, the rational procedure is first to make direct visual observations, selecting for comparison just those features which are known to have taxonomic value for the problem in hand. In many cases differences or resemblances may be so obtrusive as to obviate the need for statistical methods altogether. On the other hand, if differences and resemblances are not immediately apparent on visual inspection, special *ad hoc* measurements and indices may then be devised in order to test those characters which can reasonably be expected to be of value in the assessment of systematic affinities in any particular case. Only negative results are to be anticipated if routine measurements of little or no taxonomic value are employed.

THE FALLACY OF TREATING CHARACTERS SEPARATELY AND INDEPENDENTLY INSTEAD OF IN COMBINATION

This fallacy has recently been treated in some detail by Bronowski and Long (13, 14). They point out that a bone or a tooth is a unit and not a discrete assembly of independent measurements, and that to consider their measurements singly is likely to be both inconclusive and misleading. The right statistical method, they emphasize, must treat the set of variates as a single coherent matrix. This can be done by the technique of multivariate analysis, which is essentially a method (not possible with more elementary techniques) that can be used for comparing morphological *patterns*. In principle, the application of the technique is straightforward enough, but it requires care and discrimination, a sound knowledge of morphology, and also a considerable experience of statistical methods. A number of measurements or indices of a bone or tooth are selected, which are judged on morphological grounds to be taxonomically significant; and from these the averages, variances, and correlations for a number of specimens are calculated. It is then possible to construct a numerical picture of the size and shape of the bone or tooth (and of the extent to which they vary), and to express this as a discriminant function. Such functions may be used for deciding whether (say) a fossil hominoid tooth is more likely to belong to a pongid or a hominid type, provided, of course, that the particular discriminant functions already calculated for the two families are sufficiently distinct. Bronowski and Long have emphasized the value of multivariate analysis by applying it to a controversial issue which had arisen in regard to certain teeth of the fossil genus *Australopithecus* found in South Africa, and they were able to resolve the controversy by demonstrating very positively their hominid character (see p. 153).

THE FALLACY OF INADEQUATE OR INACCURATE
STATISTICAL TREATMENT

This fallacy has been dealt with in part in the preceding section. The possibility of inaccuracies of computation is one which needs to be borne in mind, for cases have occurred in which such errors have led to rather serious misstatements and misunderstanding. The amateur statistician needs to check and recheck his calculations so that there can be no possible doubt about the accuracy of his final figures. One of the disadvantages of scientific papers which incorporate elaborate statistical analyses is that, since only the end results of the calculations are usually published, the latter cannot be checked by the reader. It is not a little disconcerting to contemplate the possibility that simple errors of calculation have occasionally occurred in the biometrical work of the nonprofessional statistician, leading to results the falsity of which may not become apparent for some time.

THE PRINCIPLE OF MORPHOLOGICAL EQUIVALENCE IN MAKING STATISTICAL COMPARISONS

Failure to understand this principle is perhaps one of the most serious sources of fallacy likely to affect statistical studies by those who are not thoroughly acquainted with the morphology of the skeletal elements with which they are dealing. A simple (but rather crude) example may be offered by referring to a measurement often employed in craniology—the auricular height. This is commonly taken by measuring the maximum height of the skull (in the Frankfurt plane)[2] from the auditory aperture; and in comparing different racial groups of *H. sapiens* it gives an index of the height of the brain case at this particular level. But, in comparing *H. sapiens* with (say) the gorilla, it would clearly be misleading to employ the same technique, for in male gorillas the height of the skull is often considerably extended by the development of a powerful sagittal crest. If such a comparison were made, it would be a comparison of the height of the brain case in *H. sapiens* with the height of the brain case *plus* a sagittal crest in the gorilla and would have no meaning from the morphological viewpoint. This is, of course, an extreme example, but it is perhaps not fully realized that similar (if less obvious) fallacies may be incurred in other craniometric work in which over-all measurements of the skull are commonly equated with one another. In comparing skulls of closely related groups, such measurements may be sufficiently equivalent morphologically to make direct metrical comparisons valid. But if they are used to compare, say, a modern European skull with the skull of the fossil species, *H. erectus*, quite serious difficulties are involved. For example, in the European the glabello-maximal length is an ap-

[2] The Frankfurt plane, and also some of the anatomical landmarks of the skull to which reference is made in the text, are illustrated in Fig. 2, p. 33.

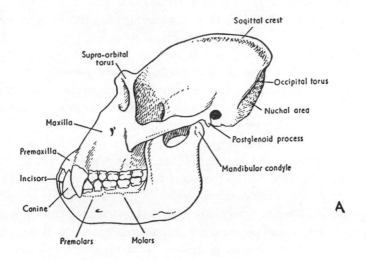

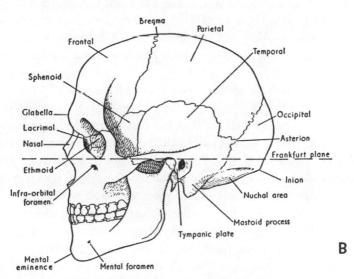

Fig. 2.—The skull of a male gorilla (*A*) and of modern *Homo sapiens* (*B*) seen from the side, to illustrate some of the anatomical landmarks to which reference is made in the text.

proximate measurement of the maximal length of the brain case. But in the skull of *H. erectus* it measures a good deal more, for the glabello-maximal length is complicated by the exaggerated development of a massive supra-orbital torus, the great thickness of the skull, and the projection backward of an exaggerated occipital torus. The over-all glabello-maximal measurement is thus not strictly comparable (in the morphological sense) with that of a European skull—in both cases it involves a number of different elements which may be independently variable among themselves. Again, in the European skull the maximal width is commonly situated in the parietal region, while in the *Homo erectus* skull it is situated in the temporal region (see Fig. 16, p. 148). Thus to compare the maximal width in the two skulls is to compare measurements which are also not morphologically equivalent. In fairness to physical anthropologists generally, it must be stated that these sources of fallacy in comparative osteometric studies are usually quite well recognized, but this may not always be the case with the less careful workers. As a further example we may take the lower front premolar tooth in the Hominidae and Pongidae. One method which has been used for measuring the length of this tooth is to take the maximal anteroposterior diameter in the axis of the tooth row. But, as is well known, in the anthropoid apes the front lower premolar is commonly rotated on its vertical axis, so that the axis corresponding morphologically to the transverse axis of the hominid premolar is directed obliquely posteromedially. Thus, to compare the maximal anteroposterior diameters in the axis of the tooth row in the two groups is to compare dimensions of the premolar itself which again are not morphologically comparable. What is actually being compared in this case is the maximal anteroposterior *space* occupied by the premolar in the tooth row—a very different thing. In comparing over-all measurements of skeletal elements, it is of the greatest importance that the morphological basis of the dimensions to be compared should be stated very precisely indeed. It may be argued that the fallacy of morphological nonequivalence must almost necessarily be involved in any over-all measurement of a skeletal structure, since such a measurement is bound to include a number of different components which may vary independently. For example, two skulls may show the same thickness of cranial wall, but the latter may actually be composed of different proportions of the outer table, inner table, and diploë. This, of course, is perfectly true, but it only serves to emphasize still more strongly the need for care in stating the morphological fundamentals of the biometric data employed.

The amateur biometrician, when comparing bones or teeth of different shapes, has sometimes fallen into the trap of comparing dimensions which (because of the different shape) are not morphologically comparable and then, on the basis of this false comparison, may conclude that because these dimensions are similar the bones or teeth are actually of the *same* shape. We may reiterate here (what has already been pointed out) that, while biometrical studies of immediately related forms belonging to the same restricted group (such as a species or subspecies) may be expected to give fair comparisons which approximate sufficiently closely in their morphological equivalence, the statistical comparison of different genera which show a greater disparity of form needs to be carried out with a very critical appreciation of the technical difficulties involved.[3]

THE FALLACY OF COMPARING SKELETAL ELEMENTS IN INDIVIDUALS OF DIFFERENT AGE, SEX, AND SIZE

This is a fallacy which is perhaps hardly likely to occur in the hands of careful workers—and yet it does occur from time to time. It is well recognized that age changes may lead to quite considerable modifications in the structural details and proportions of skeletal elements. In the skull, for example, they are so marked that it would clearly be fallacious to compare a few measurements of the adult skull of a primitive hominid with those of juvenile skulls of an anthropoid ape and to infer from such a comparison that the former is not markedly different from anthropoid apes in general. In regard to sex differences, again, it

[3] The fallacies which may arise from the comparison of over-all measurements in types which are not closely related have previously been emphasized by Washburn (147).

would obviously be misleading to compare the dimensions of the canine teeth in fossil hominoids of presumably male sex with the relatively small teeth of a female gorilla and to conclude therefrom that, in these particular dimensions, the fossil teeth fall within the range of variation of those of Recent apes. The sex variation needs to be taken into account in such a case, as it does also in comparisons of morphological and metrical features of the skull and skeleton in general.

The factor of body size in statistical comparisons is perhaps of even greater importance, for the reason that it has been overlooked much more frequently by physical anthropologists. Differences of proportions in the skull and skeleton in Primates of different size may be merely an expression of allometric growth, or they may be related to the mechanical requirements dependent on differences in body weight. In either case, of course, they may be of very little taxonomic importance (except perhaps in the determination of specific or subspecific distinctions). Thus in quadrupedal mammals the relative thickness of the leg bones is a function of the absolute size of the animal, for the strength of a bone as a supporting structure varies as its cross-sectional area (i.e., as the square of the linear dimensions of the animal), while the weight of the animal varies as the volume (i.e., as the cube of the linear dimensions). In heavier mammals, therefore, the leg bones are relatively thick, and their actual shape may thus be markedly different from those of lightly built (but still quite closely related) types. Clearly, then, it may be very misleading to compare the "robusticity index" of (say) the femur in Primates of very different body size (e.g., hominids, apes, and monkeys) and then assume degrees of affinity or divergence without any reference at all to the body-size factor. The differences in shape of bones may be even more accentuated by the fact that in larger animals the muscular ridges, tuberosities, and so forth are much more powerfully developed. Nor does this difficulty apply only to limb bones. In the skull it is well known that in closely related animals account must be taken of the factor of allometry in comparing relative size of brain case and relative size of jaws; and variations in the proportion and indices of these structures may again be reflected in differences depending on the degree of development of muscular ridges or of bony features which have developed in response to mechanical stresses. Thus, for example, it would be futile to compare cranial indices of a gorilla with those of a small monkey, with any idea of drawing taxonomic conclusions, unless factors of body size are first taken into account. For the same reason (though at first sight the case is a less obvious one) it would be misleading to make a direct comparison of cranial indices in the small and delicately built skull of a pygmy chimpanzee with those of a large and massive skull of a fossil *Australopithecus*. And even in comparisons of modern human skulls of a single homogeneous series, account needs to be taken of absolute size, for it is well established by biometrical studies that there is a significant correlation between form (as expressed in cranial indices) and absolute size.

It can hardly be overemphasized that in comparing dimensions and indices of skull, limb bones, pelvis, or other skeletal elements of Primates generally, taxonomic conclusions must first be preceded by an inquiry into all the complicating factors related to body size, an inquiry which may need elaborate statistical studies and which most certainly requires an intimate knowledge of the structural responses of skeletal elements to functional demands.

THE FALLACY OF COMPARING MEASUREMENTS TAKEN BY DIFFERENT OBSERVERS USING DIFFERENT TECHNIQUES

The dangers of this fallacy have been emphasized again and again by biometricians, and the only excuse for mentioning it here is that it is still overlooked by some writers. If it is certain that the different observers are using identical techniques for recording their measurements, the latter may be employed for comparative studies; but they still need to be used with the greatest circumspection (particularly in the case of very small objects, where measurements need to be accurate to a fraction of a millimeter). Where it is apparent that different observers are not employing precisely the same techniques, statistical comparisons must necessarily be stultified. In anthropological craniometry attempts have been made (with some success) to secure general agreement on the definitions of points and planes which serve as a basis for statistical measurements (see, for example, Buxton and Morant, 25). In regard to some of the other elements of the skeleton and also the dentition, the virtual absence of standardization of metrical technique renders comparisons between different observers very hazardous indeed.

THE FALLACY OF RELYING FOR ASSESSMENT OF AFFINITIES
ON BIOMETRICAL ANALYSIS OF CHARACTERS WHICH
MAY HAVE NO GENETIC BASIS

It is not always recognized by anthropologists that, during the period of growth, bone is a very plastic material. That is to say, its form may be readily modified by the mechanical effects of pressure and traction of the soft parts immediately related to it and also by the effects of dietetic deficiencies or constitutional disturbances of one sort or another. This needs to be taken into account as a possible source of fallacy in the attempts which have sometimes been made to assess the affinities of the various racial groups of *H. sapiens* on the basis of osteometric data, particularly in those cases where differences are so slight as to be detected only by statistical methods. So far as paleoanthropology is concerned, also, it is a factor which always needs to be taken into account when seeking evidence for the differentiation of geographical variants of the same general type. For example, it has been argued that the Javanese and Chinese representatives of the Pleistocene species *H. erectus* are taxonomically distinct because (*inter alia*) the thigh bone of the latter shows a flattening of the shaft (*platymeria*) which is not present in the former. But, apart from the fact that this is a feature which shows considerable variation within the limits of the single species *H. sapiens,* there is some suggestive evidence of an indirect nature that the degree of flattening of the shaft may depend on nutritional factors (24). If this is so, it is not a genetic character which can be properly used for taxonomic reference. How far nutritional or other postnatal influences may determine minor differences in cranial or facial proportions is still quite uncertain. It is for this reason, of

course, that in the study of modern populations physical anthropologists are now placing less reliance on the comparisons of
traditional anthropometry and are concentrating their attention
on characters whose genetic composition is directly ascertainable
and by reference to which racial groups can be classified objectively on the basis of gene frequencies.

8. The Importance of Geological Age for Determining the Evolutionary Position of Fossils

It is necessary to recognize the distinction between a morphological series linking one taxonomic group with another and a
geological series representing a true temporal sequence. A graded
morphological series, by itself, may be of direct importance in the
determination of major taxonomic groupings, and it may also provide indirect evidence of great value for a provisional assessment
of phylogenetic relationships. But evolutionary lines of development can be finally determined only by the demonstration of an
actual temporal sequence, and the latter can be established only
if geological dating is secure. It is necessary to emphasize that
anatomical studies *by themselves* can, of course, provide no basis
for assessing geological age—this must depend on the studies of
geologists based on stratigraphic data and the estimation of radioactive and other chemical elements in fossilized remains, of paleontologists based on faunal evidence, and of archeologists based
on cultural sequences. Of these different lines of evidence, that
provided by geological data is undoubtedly the most important,
for paleontological and archeological evidence of the antiquity
of fossilized remains is essentially derivative, being itself ultimately based on geological evidence. So far as hominid paleontology is concerned, it is unfortunate that the geological evidence
of antiquity has in the past so often been equivocal, mainly for
the reason that the fossil remains were discovered by chance and
the stratigraphic evidence obscured before there had been an
opportunity for a systematic study of the site, or they were found
in the course of excavations by workers who were not qualified
by training and experience to assess the geological evidence.

Undoubtedly many of the unsatisfying controversies which in

the past have been aroused by the discovery of hominid fossils might have been avoided, had it been possible in the first instance to establish a dating with reasonable assurance. In the absence of any degree of certainty, there has been a tendency for some anatomists to select that evidence for antiquity which seems best to fit in with the morphological status of the fossil. But this is a tendency which must be strenuously avoided, for it introduces a very obvious subjective element. Naturally, if the anatomist finds from the study of a skeleton assigned to a great antiquity that it shows no significant difference from that of modern *H. sapiens,* he is entitled to issue a caveat or perhaps to demand a more rigorous inquiry into the evidence for geological age, but he is not entitled to ignore the evidence simply because it conflicts with his preconceived ideas of evolutionary history. On the other hand, if a fossil of primitive type is found in a deposit which is *later* in geological age than might be expected on the general evidence already available, this need not disturb conclusions previously accepted regarding its evolutionary position, for it is quite well recognized that archaic types may persist for long periods in some parts of the world after they have given rise to more advanced types elsewhere (see Fig. 1). For example, individuals of the species *H. erectus* certainly persisted into the Middle Pleistocene in the Far East, that is to say, at a time when *H. sapiens* (or the immediate precursor of this species) was already in existence in Europe. A parallel example is also to be found in the evolutionary history of the Equidae, for some representatives of the genus *Parahippus* are known to have survived into the Upper Miocene, although other representatives of the *same* genus had already given rise to the succeeding phase of equid evolution (*Merychippus*) by the Middle Miocene.

These considerations have reference to a very common source of confusion and needless argumentation in discussions on evolution (and particularly on hominid evolution) when the suggestion is made that a particular fossil type may be "ancestral" to a later type. Thus, if the proposition is put forward that *H. erectus* is ancestral to *H. sapiens,* this does not, of course, mean (though some critics have evidently supposed it to mean) that the particular individuals whose remains have actually been found in Java or China are claimed to be the direct ancestors of *H. sapiens,* or even that the local group or subspecies of which they are representatives included direct ancestors. It means only to suggest that the species as a whole provided the matrix which gave rise— perhaps elsewhere in the world and perhaps at an earlier time— to the precursors of *H. sapiens.* Or, to put it another way, it means that, so far as their probable morphological characters can be inferred indirectly from comparative anatomical and paleontological studies and also by analogy with what is known of the evolutionary history of other mammalian groups, the ancestors of *H. sapiens* would have resembled the known individuals of the *H. erectus* group so closely as not to be specifically distinguishable. Similarly, when it is suggested that *Australopithecus* may be ancestral to later hominids (and on the purely morphological evidence the suggestion is a perfectly valid one), it is not implied that the representatives of this genus found in Africa are themselves the actual ancestors. The fact is that in their anatomical structure the African fossils conform so closely to theoretical postulates for an intermediate phase of early hominid evolution (based on indirect evidence) as to lead to the inference that the actual ancestral group could hardly be *generically* distinct. It is here a question of weighing the available evidence and estimating probabilities. Only when the paleontological record becomes more fully documented by further discoveries will it be permissible to make more definite statements on these particular problems. But, in any case, the chances of finding the fossil remains of *actual* ancestors, or even representatives of the local geographical group which provided the actual ancestors, are so fantastically remote as not to be worth consideration.

9. PRIMITIVE (OR GENERALIZED) AND SPECIALIZED CHARACTERS

In discussions on possible relationships of certain fossil hominids to *H. sapiens,* the argument is sometimes advanced that they are too specialized in one or another anatomical feature to have provided an ancestral basis for modern types. The suggestion here, of course, is that the development of some morphological character which is not present in *H. sapiens,* and wherein the latter appears to preserve a more primitive condition, implies an aberrant specialization which precludes any consideration of an ancestral relationship. In order to discuss the validity of such arguments, it is clear that we need some definition of the terms "primitive or generalized" and "specialized," and we also need to consider whether a structural specialization by itself necessarily implies the impossibility of reversion to a supposedly more primitive condition.

In studies of phylogenesis the distinction between morphological characters which are essentially primitive or generalized and those which may be regarded as divergent or specialized is commonly based on several considerations. In the first place, a study of the comparative anatomy of living types, particularly of those which, on the whole, are the most simply organized and occupy the most lowly position in a scale of increasing elaboration, may give an indirect indication of the relation between primitive and specialized features. A reference to the earlier fossil representatives of the group will provide further evidence which may, indeed, be conclusive if the fossil record is sufficiently complete to provide a closely graded sequence of evolutionary development. Detailed anatomical studies of the morphological characters concerned, with special reference to their embryological development, may add still further information. As a simple and very obvious example, we may take the morphological character of pentadactyly. This is judged to be a primitive and generalized condition in mammals which has in some cases been replaced by specializations depending on the loss of one or more digits; the reasons for this assumption are as follows: In living mammals of a simple organization, and also in Reptilia (from which mammals were originally derived), pentadactyly is the general rule; paleontology has demonstrated that in the early precursors of those mammals which today have less than five digits pentadactyly was also a characteristic feature; and, lastly, a detailed anatomical study of mammals with less than five digits may reveal, in the adult, vestigial remains of those which have been lost in the course of evolution or, in the embryo, transient traces of these vanished structures.

By the application of criteria such as these, it is usually possible to determine which characters can be designated as primitive or generalized and which are obvious specializations. For example, so far as the Hominoidea are concerned, it is certain that the gross elongation of the forelimbs in the Recent anthropoid apes (associated with retrogressive changes in the pollex and modifications of the limb musculature) are specializations from the primitive or generalized Primate condition. The same may also be said of the profound modifications of the skull and skeleton for erect bipedalism in the Hominidae. It may also be accepted, by the same line of reasoning, that the brachydont canine or the retrogressive changes in the last molar of *H. sapiens* are specialized features.

The importance of making a general distinction between primitive and specialized characters depends on the fact that the latter may be taken to indicate divergent trends of evolution, giving rise to more or less aberrant groups, and such aberrant groups, of course, are unlikely to bear an ancestral relationship to later-evolved groups in which similar specializations are absent. This consideration introduces us again to the much discussed question of the irreversibility of evolution. As already mentioned (p. 17), there is no need to debate this question here, for it has been adequately discussed elsewhere. The important point to recognize is that, while the principle of the irreversibility of evolution is perfectly sound in its general application, it is not legitimate to use it as an argument against ancestral relationships in reference to isolated characters which may have quite a simple genetic basis and which are not obviously related to any marked degree of *functional* specialization. It is well known that some mutational processes may be reversible, for this has actually been demonstrated by genetic studies in the laboratory. It is also certain that individual morphological or metrical characters considered as isolated abstractions may undergo an evolutionary reversal; for example, the size of a tooth may increase and subsequently undergo a secondary reduction again (as demonstrated in the paleon-

43

tological record of the Equidae), or muscles may be developed as new morphological units and later disappear when the functional demand for them ceases to exist (as demonstrated by vestigial or atavistic appearances sometimes seen in the human body). Instances of the loss of a character previously acquired are common enough in paleontology and may be termed "negative reversals" of evolution. On the other hand, a "positive reversal," that is to say, the re-acquirement of a complicated or composite morphological character in its *exact* original form after it has been lost in the course of evolution must certainly be a rarity. For if the initial development of such a character has been the result of a multiplicity of mutations or of a prolonged sequence of successive mutations, and if it has also been dependent on a great complexity of selective influences, the chances of its redevelopment will be so entirely remote as to be discounted altogether as a possibility. Reference may also be made to the line of argument followed by Ford (45), who points out that, as any evolving group becomes more and more specialized in adaptation to one particular mode of life, the possible variations which could be of use to it become progressively restricted. "Finally," he goes on to say, "it attains a state of 'orthogenesis' in which the only changes open to the species are those which push it along the path it has already pursued." In other words, it becomes more and more difficult, on the basis of the natural selection of heritable variations, for an evolving line to retrace its steps and thus reverse its evolutionary trends. It need hardly be said that, in using the term "orthogenesis," Ford is not referring here to the effects of an inherent tendency within the organism to evolve in a certain direction, but to the effects of what has been called "orthoselection."

But, while it is legitimate to exclude from ancestral relationship to modern types any fossil group which provides clear morphological evidence of an aberrant development obviously related to any extreme functional specialization, it is equally important to avoid the assumption that any minor deviation from a supposedly primitive condition must necessarily also be exclusive in the same sense. For example, it has been suggested that the development of a sagittal crest on the skull of some of the Australo-

pithecinae from South and East Africa (see p. 146) would debar
these fossil types from consideration as possible ancestors of *Homo*.
But there is no evidence that a sagittal crest is a morphological entity having a separate genetic basis; it is no more than the secondary result of a growth process depending on the combination of a
small brain case with large jaws and large temporal muscles (it is
"built up" by the further extension upward of these muscles when
they have reached the limits of the cranial roof at the mid-line of
the skull). Indeed, it is a character which would be expected to
be present in the earlier, small-brained representatives of the
Hominidae, for only as a result of the later expansion of the brain
(and the concomitant reduction of the jaws), would the temporal
muscles during growth find adequate accommodation on the
brain case itself without the need to build up a sagittal crest. It
has also been argued that the Pleistocene hominid species *H. erectus* could not be ancestral to *H. sapiens* because it was characterized by prominent supra-orbital ridges which are absent in *H. sapiens* and were presumably absent in the evolutionary precursors
of the Hominoidea. But it is too hazardous to draw such conclusions on such slender evidence; for, again, there is no theoretical
or practical reason why, in the hominid sequence of evolution, the
development and subsequent disappearance of prominent supra-
orbital ridges should not be correlated with changing proportions
of the jaws and brain case. And, in any case, nothing is known of
the genetic basis of this particular morphological character.

Granted that single mutations are reversible in direction and
that negative reversals are common phenomena of evolution, the
question arises—how are we to determine from the study of the
fossilized remains of a group of hominoids whether it has already
attained to such a degree of specialization in its anatomical structure that it must be regarded as a divergent or aberrant group
having no ancestral relationship to modern types? Surely, here it
is a matter of assessing the total morphological pattern in terms of
the probable complexity of its genetic constitution and of gauging
the degree to which morphological changes may have committed
the group to a mode of life which has restricted too far the opportunities for selection in other evolutionary directions. Thus, for

example, the structural adaptations of the modern anthropoid apes for a brachiating mode of arboreal life—as shown in the modifications of the limb skeleton and musculature—have evidently become too extreme and too complex to permit them (with any probability) to revert to the more generalized structure which would be a necessary prelude for modifications in the opposite direction of erect bipedalism. On the other hand, the large size of the molar teeth of the Australopithecinae and the heavy supraorbital ridges of *H. erectus* could certainly not be regarded as functional specializations of this type. Incidentally, the functional aspect of specialization is perhaps more important for taxonomy than is often realized; for, in the assessment of phylogenetic relationships, taxonomists have sometimes tended to lay more stress on what are presumed to be nonadaptive characters than on obviously adaptive characters. But, in the first place, it has been questioned whether a character ever is nonadaptive in the sense that it has no relation whatever to the functional demands of the environment. It is true that *by itself* a character may have no selective advantage, but it may be linked genetically with some other character which has. Second, a character which has no selective advantage may much more easily undergo a rapid change by mutational variations than one which is directly adapted to a special environment, for any sudden disturbance of the second type of character might be presumed to place the animal at an immediate disadvantage. In other words, it might be expected that, in a given environment, obviously adaptive characters would actually be more stable and therefore of more importance for assessing affinities.

We may formulate the general proposition, then, that if a fossil group shows structural changes which are evidently related to (and responsible for) functional specializations, and if the latter appear to have definitely committed it to one special mode of life, it is to the highest degree unlikely that the group would be capable of a true evolutionary reversal. That is not to say, of course, that a specialized group of animals is incapable of changing its mode of life. For example, in the course of evolution an arboreal group may become adapted for terrestrial life and subsequently become adapted again for arboreal life. But in doing so, it does not revert to the more primitive or generalized structure of its arboreal ancestors. Its terrestrial specializations are preserved and still further modified away from the primitive condition to allow such a functional transformation. Apart from functional considerations, however, it is also legitimate to discount the possibility of an evolutionary reversal if the morphological divergence from a more primitive condition can be assumed, on the basis of paleontological evidence, to be the cumulative effect of a long succession of small mutational variations exposed to selective influences of a complex nature, or if there is reason to suppose (by analogy from genetic studies of living forms) that the morphological character concerned is the phenotypical expression of a genotype which is so complex that an evolutionary reversal could occur only as the result of a multiplicity of mutational reversals.

In spite of what has been said, it needs to be emphasized that the ultimate decision as to whether a fossil genus is ancestral to a Recent genus or not must be determined by the paleontological record, and this can be done only when the latter is known in sufficient detail. On purely morphological grounds (and without reference to the paleontological sequence), there is no certain argument why the somewhat aberrant species *H. neanderthalensis* could not be ancestral to *H. sapiens*. But in this particular instance (see p. 75), the fossil record shows with reasonable probability that such was not the case. Some of the early Miocene genera of the Pongidae may have been ancestral to the Hominidae—there likewise appears to be no valid morphological argument against this. But the solution of this particular problem must depend on the amplification of the fossil record by further discoveries.

10. GENERAL CONSIDERATIONS

We have been concerned in this chapter to draw attention to some of the more obvious sources of confusion which all too commonly lead to misunderstandings and misrepresentations in discussions on hominid evolution. Undoubtedly, the failure to recognize the phylogenetic implications of taxonomic terminology has

47

been responsible for much of this confusion, for the reason that there has been a tendency to use this terminology as though it were based on morphological definitions applied to living forms only. The loose employment of colloquial group terms is an even greater source of confusion. It is a remarkable fact that even in strictly scientific papers authors frequently use the terms "man" and "human" without any attempt to define them, and it is clear, also, that they are used with very different meanings not only by different writers but also by the same writer in different contexts. The term "hominid," again, seems to be used quite frequently as though it referred only to the large-brained genus *Homo,* whereas it should be strictly employed only as the adjectival form of the taxonomic term "Hominidae." In other words, as we have tried to emphasize, it should be equated with the other familial categories of mammalian classification and apply to the whole sequence of evolution which led to the development of *Homo* (and other hominid genera) from the time when this sequence became segregated from the related family Pongidae.

The assessment of genetic affinity by the comparison of morphological details of no more than portions of a fossilized skeleton (particularly if these are very fragmentary) obviously poses a most serious problem, for in many cases such comparative studies can lead only to inconclusive results. Yet, because of its rarity, it is a matter of importance that all fossil Primate material should be subjected to intensive study and that some attempt should be made to assess the taxonomic status of each specimen, even though this may lead to no more than a provisional interpretation of its affinities. In the absence of an abundant fossil record, conclusions regarding lines of phylogenetic development must always be provisional; and, as the evidence accrues with new discoveries, they will need constant revision. Paleontologists themselves are quite aware of this, but it would be well that those less experienced in the study of fossils should recognize it also. For it is interesting to note in the literature of paleoanthropology that the polemical articles which seem so often to be evoked by new discoveries of primitive hominid fossils are contributed not so much by those with practical experience of paleontology as by those in allied fields who may even have no personal acquaintance with the fossil material under discussion. In any case, however, it can hardly be emphasized too strongly that, in assessing the taxonomic position of a fossil specimen, account must be taken of the total morphological pattern (and not its individual units) which provides the reliable morphological evidence on which zoölogical relationships can be determined. The comparison of individual characters independently as isolated abstractions, instead of treating them as integrated components of a complex pattern, is perhaps one of the main causes of the multiplicity of systems of classification of the Primates which are still to be found in the literature.

CHAPTER II

Homo

1. THE ANTIQUITY OF *Homo sapiens* AND THE PROBLEM OF NEANDERTHAL MAN

It is now generally agreed that all the modern races of mankind are variants of one species, *Homo sapiens*. So far as skeletal characters are concerned (and these, of course, are the only anatomical characters available to the paleontologist), this species may be provisionally defined[1] as follows:

A species of the genus *Homo* characterized by a mean cranial capacity of about 1,350 cc.; muscular ridges on the cranium not strongly marked; a rounded and approximately vertical forehead; supra-orbital ridges usually moderately developed and in any case not forming a continuous and uninterrupted torus; rounded occipital region with a nuchal area of relatively small extent; foramen magnum facing directly downward; the consistent presence of a prominent mastoid process of pyramidal shape (in juveniles as well as adults), associated with a well-marked digastric fossa and occipital groove; maximum width of the calvaria usually in the parietal region and axis of glabello-maximal length well above the level of the external occipital protuberance; marked flexion of the sphenoidal angle, with a mean value of about 110°; jaws and teeth of relatively small size, with retrogressive features in the last molars; maxilla having a concave facial surface, including a canine fossa; distinct mental eminence; eruption of permanent canine commonly preceding that of the second molar; spines of

[1] The diagnoses of species and genera which are offered in this thesis are intended to be provisional only. It is hoped that they may be taken as a basis of discussion for international agreement among paleoanthropologists, in order to avoid the confusions and misunderstandings which in the past have so frequently marred discussions on the origin of man.

50

cervical vertebrae (with the exception of the seventh) usually rudimentary; appendicular skeleton adapted for a fully upright posture and gait; limb bones relatively slender and straight.

On the basis of the total morphological pattern comprised by these skeletal characters (and also on the basis of biometric comparisons of over-all dimensions and of indices constructed therefrom), it is possible to affirm that the populations of late Paleolithic times, so far as they are known from fossilized remains, all conform entirely with *H. sapiens*. In other words, the species extends back in time at least as far as the beginning of the Aurignacian phase of Paleolithic culture,[2] and this, at a conservative estimate, means an antiquity of some 30,000 years. There is no known anatomical feature whereby the skeletal remains of Aurignacian (or Magdalenian) man can be distinguished from modern man, and, as is well known, the populations in Europe at this early time had already developed a highly complex culture.

Apart from the problem of the antiquity of *H. sapiens* as a species is the problem of the antiquity of the modern races of mankind as distinct geographical varieties. The definition of the word "race" is still a matter for acute discussion among anthropologists, and the loose employment of the term in common parlance, as well as the insinuations which have been linked with it by exponents of extreme political creeds, has not made it easy to secure agreement on this matter. It has to be recognized, moreover, that in zoölogical taxonomy generally there is still no complete agreement on the definition of the term "species," let alone the definition of infra-specific categories, such as "demes," "geographical races," and "subspecies." In any case the application of these terms is bound to be somewhat arbitrary; for, on evolutionary principles, each of the hierarchical systems of categories must grade insensibly into another. In the course of evolution, local groups, isolated by geographical or other barriers, will tend to undergo a gradual genetic diversification until they are sufficiently distinct to justify recognition as different demes or races. With

2 A table showing the probable relationships of successive Paleolithic cultures to the glacial and interglacial periods of the Pleistocene is shown in Fig. 3, p. 52.

continued isolation, the latter acquire a more contrasted genetic differentiation which may be expressed by placing them in separate subspecific categories. A continuation of the same process leads ultimately to the establishment of separate species which are genetically incompatible to the extent that they are no longer capable of freely interbreeding. Thus, in the evolutionary sense, a geographical race is a potential subspecies, and a subspecies is a potential species. Since all the available evidence shows that in the course of progressive differentiation the transition from lower to higher categories in the taxonomic scale is a gradual one, it is not to be expected that these categories can be defined with any clear-cut precision. If the definition of a subspecies offered by

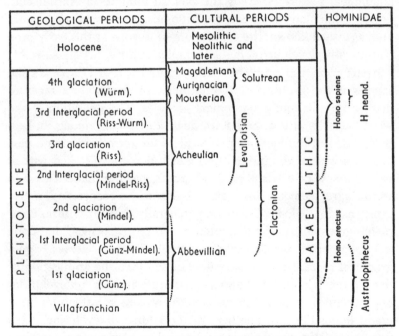

FIG. 3.—Table showing the probable relationships of successive paleolithic cultures and of different types of the Hominidae to the glacial and interglacial periods of the Pleistocene. It should be noted that these periods lasted for varying lengths of time. The second interglacial period, for example, was much more prolonged than the first and third, and the Villafranchian period may have lasted as long as the whole of the rest of the Pleistocene. For further amplification of paleolithic cultures, reference should be made to *Man the Toolmaker* by K. P. Oakley (Chicago: University of Chicago Press [1962]).

Mayr (89) is accepted, i.e., a geographically localized subdivision of the species which differs genetically and taxonomically from other subdivisions of the species, then the major races of mankind today are properly to be regarded as subspecies (equivalent, that is to say, with subspecies of other vertebrate species).[3] Of course, in recent centuries the factor of geographical isolation has become grossly disturbed, with the result that interbreeding (particularly along regions of territorial overlap) has produced intergradations between one major race and another and thus has tended to obscure genetic and phenotypic contrasts which must at one time have been more abrupt. A similar process of hybridization between subspecies among animals in the wild state is well recognized by zoölogists. For example, instances have been recorded among birds where, following a breakdown of ecological barriers or other isolating mechanisms, two closely related subspecies freely interbreed, with the resulting development of new hybrids. In the course of time such a process may obliterate subspecific differences which formerly existed; but this, of course, does not invalidate the application of the term "subspecies" in reference to the interbreeding communities while the latter still exist in the main as recognizably distinct groups.

The determination of the evolutionary differentiation of the major races of *H. sapiens* presents exceptionally difficult problems for the paleontologist. These races may be distinctive enough in the flesh, but the anatomical distinction between one and another is not reflected to anything like the same degree in the bones. While they are recognizable by a number of external (and seemingly rather superficial) characters, such as skin color, hair texture, and nose form, they are by no means so easily distinguishable by reference to skeletal characters alone—at least, not in the

[3] Some zoölogists, arguing from the definition of a *species* as a taxonomic group which, if it does interbreed with a related species, does not usually produce fertile offspring, would limit the application of the term *subspecies* to groups already sufficiently distinct genetically to impose difficulties which prevent (or, at any rate, limit) full hybridization. Such a definition clearly does not apply to all those groupings which are accorded subspecific rank by zoölogists. On the other hand, if the definition is accepted, the major races of mankind are probably to be regarded as something less distinct than subspecies.

case of individual and isolated specimens (which are usually all that paleoanthropology has to offer). It may, indeed, be possible to identify a skull of a modern Negro, an Australian aboriginal, or a European, in individual cases where the racial characters are exceptionally well marked; but the variation within each group is so great that skulls of each type may be found which are impossible of racial diagnosis. This difficulty may be illustrated by reference to the well-known skulls from the late Paleolithic sites of Grimaldi near Mentone and Chancelade in the Dordogne valley, on the significance of which there has in the past been considerable controversy.

The Grimaldi skulls had been held by many anthropologists to be quite definitely Negroid in type, and they were commonly accepted as good evidence of the existence of a Negroid race in Europe during Aurignacian times. Yet others, also from a study of the actual remains, have pronounced categorically that they show no real evidence of Negroid affinities but are simply variants of the "Mediterranean race" which now inhabits southern Europe. The Chancelade skull, of Magdalenian age, had been compared by the famous anatomist Testut with that of an Eskimo, and this diagnosis was accepted by many reputable anthropologists. This conclusion, again, has been vigorously denied by equally distinguished anthropologists, who maintain that it is but a variant of the Cro-Magnon type of *H. sapiens*. Now it is probable that there are no racial types in which the skull characters are more distinctive than Negroes and Eskimos; and yet experts fail to agree when faced with single skulls whose claims to these types are in question. If a decision proves so difficult in such cases, it will be realized how much more difficult, or even impossible, it will be to identify, by reference to limited skeletal remains, minor racial groups with less distinctive characters.

If there are difficulties in the identification of the skeletal remains of the fully differentiated racial types of today, these are very much enhanced when attempts are made to detect corresponding racial differences in prehistoric remains in which the characteristic racial traits were presumably much less developed. Yet it has been argued by some anthropologists, on the basis of such ancient fossils, that the primary races of mankind had already begun their divergent differentiation as far back as the beginning of Pleistocene times (see p. 85). While there is no inherent improbability in such a thesis, the anatomical evidence on which it is based remains entirely inadequate. The shape of the incisor teeth and the presence of exostoses along the alveolar margin of the mandible, for example, are not sufficient to justify the conclusion that Pekin man was the forerunner of the Mongolian races to the exclusion of other racial types. There is likewise no distinctive character in the Rhodesian skull which permits the assumption that Rhodesian man was a proto-Negroid (though, in some museums, restorations of this fossil man are provided with typical Negroid features and hair of the usual Negroid type).

It has unfortunately to be recognized, then, that there is as yet no sound paleontological evidence by which the antiquity of the infra-specific groupings of modern man can be satisfactorily determined. There is certainly no evidence that modern racial differentiation had become fully established before the terminal phase of the Pleistocene period, and it seems probable that it then proceeded with considerable rapidity. The local geographical areas where, as the result of temporary isolation, the genetic diversification first occurred which gave rise to the major races are either unknown, or can only be indirectly inferred by a consideration of their present-day distribution. No fossil skeleton that is indisputably older than the end of the Pleistocene has yet been discovered which can be certainly identified as of Negroid or Mongolian stock, and the skulls of Australoid type found at Wadjak, Talgai, Cohuna, and Aitape have all been assigned a Pleistocene date on evidence which is regarded by some authorities as geologically inadequate. On the other hand, the skeletal remains of Aurignacian and Magdalenian date which have so far been discovered in Europe not only are indubitably those of *H. sapiens* but are actually not distinguishable, on present evidence, from modern Europeans. Mention should be made of a number of fossil skulls of modern human type found in Africa, China, and America and dating from the terminal phase of the Pleistocene. Most of those from Africa have been stated to be of a

"Bushmanoid" type; those from America have been compared with the modern American Indians; while a presumed family of three individuals from the Upper Pleistocene of Choukoutien (near Pekin) have been compared by Weidenreich (154) individually with Mongoloid, Melanesoid, and Eskimoid types. In fact, however, it seems that the racial affinities of all these specimens are really indeterminate on the basis of such scanty material; and it may be questioned whether the opinions of those anthropologists who have described them were not influenced by the geographical locality in which they were found.

The question now arises whether *H. sapiens* as a species has a still greater antiquity than the Upper Pleistocene. From time to time in the past, claims for a remote antiquity have been made for skulls and skeletons of modern human type. The famous Galley Hill remains—found as long ago as 1888 in Middle Pleistocene gravels of the 100-foot terrace of the Thames—were accepted for many years by some authorities as contemporaneous with the deposits from which they were disinterred. The Ipswich skeleton, found beneath 4 feet of boulder clay, was assumed to antedate the last glaciation of the Ice Age. In both these cases (as in a number of other reported discoveries of a similar character) the geological evidence of antiquity was actually quite inadequate; but, even so, it was seized with avidity by those who were particularly anxious to bolster up arguments for the remote origin of *H. sapiens*. Such arguments were even used to refute the general conception of human evolution by antievolutionists, for the latter argued that, since human remains of modern type evidently antedated more primitive types which were regarded as ancestral to *H. sapiens*, they upset the morphological sequence which was supposed to provide the essential evidence for human evolution. In the case of the Ipswich skeleton, the initial claim for its antiquity was subsequently shown to have been based on a misinterpretation of the geological evidence, and the skeleton is now regarded as a secondary interment (probably of relatively recent date). The real nature of the Galley Hill skeleton was later determined by the analysis of its fluorine content (105), from which it is now quite evident that the skeleton is also of no great antiquity —perhaps the remains of a burial in Neolithic times.

Since the method of estimating the relative age of fossil bones by fluorine analysis has proved in recent years to be so valuable, it is appropriate to make further reference to it here. Many years ago it had been demonstrated that the fluorine content of fossil bone increases with geologic age. This is due to the fact that, by a process of ionic interchange, fluorine is slowly taken up from the soil in which the bone is imbedded and becomes fixed in the form of a very stable compound, fluorapatite. The amount of fluorine found in a fossil bone thus increases with time and gives an indication of the period over which it has lain in position in a particular geologic deposit. But the amount of fluorine taken up also depends, of course, on the amount of fluorine in the soil. If the latter is rich in fluorine, any bones imbedded in it may become so rapidly saturated that a fluorine analysis is of little use in estimating its age. It must be emphasized, therefore, that the analysis permits an estimation only of the *relative* antiquity of fossil material from the same deposit. Thus it does not permit a comparison of the relative (or the absolute) antiquity of fossilized bones derived from different deposits in which the fluorine content of the soil may vary widely. But in a case where, in the *same* geologic deposit, a human skull is found in association with the skeletal remains of extinct mammals of known antiquity, the fluorine test may provide evidence of the utmost importance for determining whether they are all contemporaneous (that is to say, whether they were initially placed in the deposit at approximately the same period of time). If, on the other hand, the human skull represents part of an artificial interment at a much later time, this would at once be demonstrated by its low fluorine content as compared with indigenous fossil bones. The method of fluorine analysis has been developed and applied (particularly by Oakley, 103) in a number of doubtful and disputed discoveries of human remains to which some authorities had attributed a high antiquity.

In the case of the Galley Hill skeleton, the fluorine content was found to average 0.34 per cent. This compares with a range of

1.7–2.8 per cent in Middle Pleistocene bones from the same region, 0.9–1.4 per cent for Upper Pleistocene material, and 0.05–0.3 per cent for Holocene bones. The differences are sufficiently marked to justify the firm conclusion that the Galley Hill skeleton "was not indigenous to the Middle Pleistocene gravels in which it lay, but a burial of later date—prehistoric, but probably post-Pleistocene" (Oakley and Montagu, 105). Thus, after more than fifty years of argument this way and that on the basis of inadequate geological evidence, the question has now been finally settled by fluorine analysis, and no better example could be adduced to illustrate the value of this crucial test.[4]

Some methods that are now available for estimating with considerable accuracy the *absolute* antiquity of fossils are based on the fact that certain radioactive substances often to be found in fossil-bearing strata undergo a gradual disintegration at a known rate unaffected by normal climatic changes. One such method makes use of the disintegration of the element uranium to form helium and lead. The rate of decay in this case is very slow, one million grams of uranium producing 1/7600 gram of lead every year, but by chemical estimation of helium and lead in appropriate minerals the lapse of time since the first formation of the latter can be calculated. This uranium-lead method, however, is only applicable to very ancient deposits, but it has determined the age of certain deposits of the Miocene period (estimated approximately at about twenty million years) which has a special interest for hominid evolution, for it was during this period that large apes of a very generalized type abounded in many parts of the Old World, so generalized that some of them may well have provided the ancestral basis for the subsequent emergence of the earliest hominids.

[4] It is interesting to note that Pearson and Bell (107), as a result of their biometric studies, concluded that the Galley Hill femur is distinct from that of Recent man. However, the Recent material on which they relied for their comparison was actually limited to a sample of the seventeenth-century London population, whereas, of course, "Recent man" must be assumed to include *all* modern races, as well as Neolithic man. This conclusion of Pearson and Bell is an illustration of the fallacy of extrapolating from the special to the general in biometrics (see p. 6).

Another method more recently developed is the potassium-argon method, depending on the fact that naturally occurring potassium contains 0.01 per cent of a radioactive isotope that on decay forms calcium and argon and has a half-life of thirteen hundred million years. This has given with more precision the over-all age of Miocene deposits extending back from twelve million years ago to twenty-five million years, that of the subsequent Pliocene period extending from about one and a half to twelve million years, and the beginning of the following Pleistocene period an antiquity of about one and a half million years. And it was during the Pleistocene period that hominid evolution gradually proceeded toward the final appearance of the genus *Homo* and the species *Homo sapiens.*

Lastly, we may refer to the important radioactive carbon method. This depends on the fact that, during life, organisms contain a constant amount of radioactive carbon (carbon 14) irrespective of geographical distribution or other environmental factors, and that on death the carbon 14 disintegrates at a rate of one-half its amount in 5,568 years; thus an estimation of its quantity in organic material that is suspected to be ancient will provide good evidence of its absolute antiquity. But, because of its short half-life and the technical difficulties of estimating minute quantities, the limit of dating by this method is not more than 70,000 years. The accuracy of dating by estimating the products of decay of any radioactive element of course demands very careful attention to a number of technical details, but on the whole the results so far obtained have been remarkably consistent.

Apart altogether from those fossilized remains of *H. sapiens* whose antiquity must remain entirely dubious because they are so inadequately documented,[5] there are now available a small number of specimens apparently of this species which can be assigned with reasonable assurance to the Middle Pleistocene or the early part of the Upper Pleistocene. But before considering these,

[5] These dubious specimens include some skulls of modern type from Italy, South America, and elsewhere, to which have been attributed a vast antiquity (but which are now entirely discredited) and certain skulls and jaws from East Africa whose geological dating still needs confirmation.

attention should be given to what is regarded by some authorities as a distinct species of *Homo* (*H. neanderthalensis*), which formed rather a localized geographical group occupying the continent of Europe (and some adjacent regions) during the last glaciation of the Ice Age. It should be emphasized, however, that there is no complete agreement yet on the specific status of Neanderthal man.

2. *Homo neanderthalensis*

Since the discovery of a skull cap and portions of the limb skeleton in the Neanderthal cave (near Düsseldorf) in 1856, "Neanderthal man" has now become recognized by most anthropologists as representing a distinct group of the genus *Homo* which became differentiated probably in the latter part of the Middle Pleistocene period but did not survive the end of the Pleistocene. Following on the earlier discovery, other specimens of the same type of *Homo* have been described from a number of sites in Europe, e.g., Gibraltar, La Chapelle-aux-Saints, La Quina, Spy, La Ferrassie, Mone Circeo, Le Moustier, La Naulette, and Jersey. All these fossil specimens were almost certainly contemporaneous with the later part of the Mousterian period of Paleolithic culture[6] and were representatives of a population which lived during the first phase of the last glaciation (Würm I) of the Ice Age. This population is sometimes referred to as "Neanderthal man" or "Mousterian man" (though, actually, it is characteristic only of the later Mousterian period). The cranial characters and such elements of the postcranial skeleton as are available have been studied in very considerable detail by a number of competent anatomists, and there is a general consensus of opinion that the differences from *H. sapiens* which they show are sufficiently consistent to justify at least some degree of taxonomic distinction (see Fig. 4). The diagnostic characters of the group may be defined as follows.

The skull is distinguished by an exaggerated development of a

[6] There is some doubt about the skull found at Le Moustier, but it conforms quite closely in its anatomical features to the several other skulls of Mousterian date found in the same region in southwestern France.

massive supra-orbital torus, forming an uninterrupted shelf of bone overhanging the orbits (with complete fusion of the ciliary and orbital elements); absence of a vertical forehead; marked flattening of the cranial vault (platycephaly); relatively high position of the external occipital protuberance and the development (usually) of a strong occipital torus; a massive development of

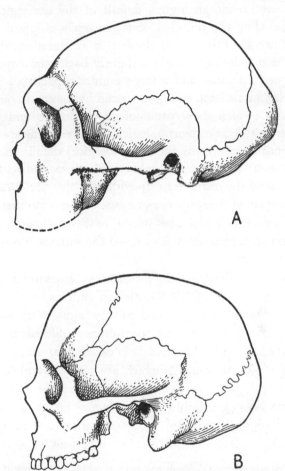

Fig. 4.—The skull of (A) *Homo neanderthalensis* (Monte Circeo) compared with (B) that of *Homo sapiens*. Approximately one-third natural size. (Pictorial comparisons of this sort naturally have the disadvantage that they compare only *individual* specimens. But they do at least convey to the reader a general idea of contrasts and similarities.) (Fig. 4, A, by courtesy of the Trustees of the British Museum.)

the nasomaxillary region of the facial skeleton, with an inflated appearance of the maxillary wall; a heavy mandible, lacking a chin eminence; a pronounced tendency of the molar teeth to taurodontism (that is, enlargement of the pulp cavity with fusion of the roots);[7] a relatively wide sphenoidal angle of the cranial base (about 130°; see Fig. 7, p. 77); angular contour of the occiput; certain morphological details of the ear region of the skull (including the rounded or transversely elliptical shape of the auditory aperture, the conformation of the mastoid process, and of the mandibular fossa); a slightly backward disposition of the foramen magnum; and a large cranial capacity (1,300-1,600 cc.).[8] The limb skeleton is characterized by the coarse build of the long bones (which show pronounced curvatures and relatively large extremities), the morphological features of the pubic bone (139), and by certain of the morphological details of the talus and calcaneus bones of the ankle, which are said to be somewhat "simian" in character. In addition, the vertebrae of the cervical region of the spine in some cases show a striking development of the spinous processes which, however, though somewhat simian in appearance, does not exceed the extreme limits of variation in *H. sapiens*.

All these morphological factors are not known for certain to have been present in all the Mousterian remains listed earlier; for some of the latter are represented only by fragmentary skulls. Here we have exemplified one of the inherent difficulties of much paleontological work—the attempt to define a taxonomic group on the basis of skeletal remains which are rarely complete (or anything like complete) in *individual* specimens. It is a difficulty, however, which constantly has to be met as best may be (even if only on a provisional basis) by reference to such material as is available up to date. Fortunately, in the present instance the total

[7] Some degree of taurodontism has been reported as an occasional variant in *H. sapiens*, though rarely showing the extreme condition to be found in some representatives of later Mousterian man. Nevertheless, the character of taurodontism *by itself* is not definitely diagnostic of *H. neanderthalensis*.

[8] For an amplification of these morphological details see Keith (61, 62), Boule and Vallois (11), and Howell (55).

morphological pattern presented by the cranial and skeletal characters just enumerated is rather distinctive; it is not to be found in any of the races of modern man. Also, very fortunately, the cranial characters have been analyzed and assessed on a statistical basis in a systematic study by Morant (92). This author emphasized a number of metrical features in which the skull differs from that of *H. sapiens*—for example, the skulls are "particularly characterized by the absolutely and relatively large size of the facial skeleton"; and a comparison of the relevant measurements is sufficient to show that the form of the facial skeleton "dissociates the type from the homogeneous one of modern man"; nearly all measurements designed to assess the sagittal flattening of the cranial vault "relegate the Mousterian skulls to positions which are entirely outside the inter-racial distributions for modern man"; the axis of the foramen magnum is more deflected from the vertical (owing to a rotation of the occipital bone) than in modern types; the skulls are "distinguished from all modern types by having a greater transverse flattening of the vault, more vertical walls and a height that is peculiarly small in proportion to the breadth"; and as regards the breadth-length indices of the separate frontal, parietal, and occipital bones, "some fall entirely outside the inter-racial range for modern skulls." Morant concludes finally that "available measurements of the skulls of Mousterian man indicate that the type was remarkably homogeneous" and that "between it and all modern racial types there is a distinct hiatus, which may be taken to indicate a specific difference." A biometrical study has more recently been made of the Neanderthal femur by Twiesselman (144). He emphasizes the remarkable homogeneity of the thigh bone (at least in the Western Neanderthal population of the last glacial period) and the differences in certain indices and dimensions from those of modern *Homo sapiens*. This study thus extends and confirms the conclusions drawn by Morant from his own study of cranial characters.

If to these distinguishing metrical characters are added the distinguishing morphological details already numerated, it seems justifiable to accord a specific rank to later Mousterian man, and for this purpose the well-recognized taxonomic category of *H.*

neanderthalensis may be conveniently employed. Certainly, the skeletal differences from *H. sapiens* are of much the same order as those which have been accepted as valid evidence of specific distinction in other groups of Primates. For example, the morphological contrast does not appear to be appreciably less than the contrast between *H. erectus* and *H. sapiens* (though of course in a somewhat different direction). The taxonomic distinction of *H. neanderthalensis* is still further emphasized by the fact that its specific characters are already manifested in the skulls of immature individuals;[9] this provides evidence of a pattern of growth which is fundamentally different from that of the skull of *H. sapiens*. The Mousterian fossil remains which are assignable to *H. neanderthalensis* on the basis of these metrical and morphological criteria seem to have represented a comparatively isolated group occupying for the most part a restricted geographical area for a limited period of time during the first (and most severe) phase of the last glaciation. Indeed, it may well have been the isolation caused by the rigorous climatic conditions which actually led to the differentiation of the species; for, as Howell (56) has noted, "under this environment selection would be severe, chance for genetic drift at an optimum, and opportunities for migration reduced to a minimum." It is to the representatives of this particular group that the term "Neanderthal man" was originally applied. But the term has also been somewhat loosely applied to human remains of still greater antiquity (contemporaneous, that is to say, with the interglacial phase preceding the Würm glaciation or even earlier), for the reason that in some of them the supra-orbital ridges are rather strongly developed and thus tend in appearance to approximate to those which form one of the characteristics of later Mousterian man. However, apart from the fact that this feature *by itself* would not provide an adequate criterion for a specific distinction, the supra-orbital ridges in the pre-Mousterian or early Mousterian representatives of *Homo* usually correspond more closely with those of *H. sapiens* in the

[9] Juvenile skulls are known from Gibraltar, La Quina, Le Moustier, and Teshik-Tash.

tendency they show to division into medial (ciliary) and lateral (orbital) elements separated by a shallow groove (sulcus supra-orbitalis). This twofold composition of the supra-orbital ridges in *H. sapiens* is well recognized in those modern races in which the ridges are strongly developed; and Howell rightly points out that in this feature some of the earlier skulls are very similar to Australian and Tasmanian skulls. In *H. neanderthalensis* of later Mousterian times, on the other hand, the ridges are specialized to form a continuous, uninterrupted *torus*.

While the skulls of the pre-Mousterian or early Mousterian population in Europe in some cases have strongly developed supra-orbital ridges and, to that extent, present a "Neanderthaloid" appearance, they lack many of the morphological features which, taken in combination with one another as components of a total morphological pattern, may be regarded as diagnostic of the species *H. neanderthalensis*. As already noted, this pattern includes such features as the absence of a vertical or well-rounded forehead, the marked degree of platycephaly, the angular occiput, and the massive jaws. On the contrary, in the earlier skulls the forehead is found to be relatively well developed, the platycephaly much less marked, the occiput is well rounded with rather weak muscular markings, and the jaws less massive (the maxillary wall having a hollowed, instead of an inflated, appearance). In other words, the skull as a whole approximates more closely to that of *H. sapiens*. In so far as they are known, also, the limb bones appear to be quite similar to those of modern man in their lighter construction and straighter shafts.

When the remains of pre-Mousterian and early Mousterian *Homo* are compared with *H. sapiens,* there seems no solid basis for making a specific distinction at all, in spite of the fact that some of them do seem to adumbrate certain of the distinctive features which later appeared in *H. neanderthalensis* and which form the basis of the taxonomic definition of this species. On the other hand, it has to be recognized that there is no sharp delimitation between early Mousterian *H. sapiens* and later Mousterian *H. neanderthalensis,* for we seem to be dealing here with an actual evolutionary series in which a morphological gradation can be demonstrated to coincide with a temporal sequence. It is to be expected, therefore, that taxonomic difficulties will arise in an attempt to classify intermediate stages of development.[10] Some authorities have suggested that Neanderthal man of later Mousterian date may conveniently be referred to as the *classic* or *extreme Neanderthal type,* and his predecessor as the *generalized Neanderthal type.* As already noted, however, there appears (on the evidence at present available) to be no sound argument for distinguishing the so-called "generalized" Neanderthal type specifically from *H. sapiens.* For this reason, the appellation "generalized Neanderthal," though convenient for reference, is likely to be misleading because it suggests a type which was antecedent only to *H. neanderthalensis.* On the contrary, the latter now appears, on the chronological evidence, to have been the product of an aberrant side line of evolution which branched off from the precursors of modern man when they had already reached a status not distinguishable morphologically as an early variety of *H. sapiens.*

It has been mentioned earlier that the evidence for an evolutionary series leading to the appearance of *H. neanderthalensis* is based partly on the demonstration of a temporal sequence of fossil remains. This was summarized by Zeuner (166) in a short review on *The Age of Neanderthal Man.* It now appears that among the fossil remains which can, with some assurance, be assigned to the last interglacial period or earlier are those found at Steinheim, Fontéchevade, Swanscombe, Ehringsdorf, Quinzano, Krapina, Saccopastore, and Mount Carmel (in part). Because of their antiquity (and the fact that they precede in time the extreme Neanderthal type), these fossils merit separate reference.

[10] We may appeal again to the evolution of the Equidae for a parallel case. Simpson (135) remarks that *"Parahippus* arose in the early Miocene from *Miohippus* and its earlier species were, of course, very like that ancestor. The transition is marked by the general establishment of characters that were already appearing in *Miohippus* as occasional variations." Precisely the same might be said of the evolutionary development of the specialized *H. neanderthalensis* from pre-Mousterian *H. sapiens.*

3. PRE-MOUSTERIAN AND EARLY MOUSTERIAN *Homo sapiens*

As noted in the preceding section, *H. neanderthalensis* of later Mousterian date was evidently a collateral development derived from an earlier population whose morphological characters hardly justify a specific separation from *H. sapiens*. The evidence for this conclusion may be briefly reviewed by reference to individual fossil specimens.

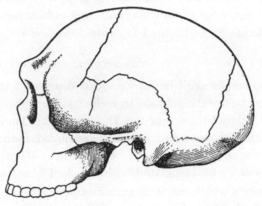

FIG. 5.—The Steinheim skull (partly restored). Approximately one-third natural size. (By courtesy of the Trustees of the British Museum.)

THE STEINHEIM SKULL

In 1933 the Steinheim skull (Fig. 5) was found near a tributary of the River Weimar (30 km. north of Stuttgart) in interglacial gravels also containing remains of *Elephas antiquus* and *Dicerorhinus merckii*. These gravels have been assigned by some to the third, and by others to the second, interglacial period. The skull is estimated to have a cranial capacity of about 1,100 cc. and shows only a moderate degree of platycephaly. It also possesses strongly developed supra-orbital ridges, which appear to adumbrate the massive ridges so characteristic of the extreme Neanderthal type of skull of later Mousterian times (160). In neither of these characters, however, does it diverge to such a degree from *H. sapiens* as to warrant a specific distinction. The ample development of the forehead region, the rounded form of the occiput (with a low and rather feebly marked external occipital protuberance), the contour in horizontal section of the nasomaxillary region (with a hollowing of the maxillary wall), the relatively moderate dimensions of the facial skeleton, and the total morphological pattern presented by the mastoid process, tympanic plate, and mandibular fossa comprise a combination of morphological features which conforms entirely with *H. sapiens* and contrasts with the skulls of *H. neanderthalensis*. The somewhat low cranial capacity, also, comes well within the range of modern man, and in this feature again the Steinheim skull does not conform with the characteristically large-brained *H. neanderthalensis*.

THE SWANSCOMBE SKULL BONES

The Swanscombe skull bones were first discovered in 1935 and 1936, 24 feet below the surface in well-stratified gravels forming part of the 100-foot terrace of the Thames (141). These are definitely interglacial deposits, and the associated fauna includes *Elephas antiquus, Dicerorhinus megarhinus, Megaceros,* and *Dama clactonia.* Also associated with the skull bones were found flint implements which can with certainty be assigned to the early Middle Acheulian hand-ax industry (Acheulian III of Breuil). The geological, archeological, and faunal evidence is all consistent with the conclusion that the skull bones date back to the Mindel-Riss interglacial period. Finally, this has received some confirmation from a fluorine analysis of the bones (103), for the latter have been found to contain 2 per cent fluorine (which equates well with the percentage found in the bones of extinct mammals indigenous to the Middle Pleistocene terrace deposits at Swanscombe). Taking all the evidence into account, it may be affirmed that in no other example of Paleolithic man is the dating more completely attested than it is in the case of the Swanscombe bones.[11]

[11] It will be agreed that, however sound the evidence for the antiquity of the Swanscombe bones may appear to be, this isolated discovery pointing to the existence of *H. sapiens* in Europe during the second interglacial period needs to be confirmed (just because it *is* an isolated discovery) by the accession of further, and more complete, material.

The Swanscombe "skull" (as it is sometimes called) consists only of the occipital and the two parietal bones (78). But these are extremely well preserved and articulate together perfectly. Since the sutures still remain open, the bones evidently belong to a young individual of probably twenty to twenty-five years. The weakness of the muscular markings suggests the female sex. A careful and extensive biometric study by Morant (94) failed to reveal any measurement or index which differentiates the "skull" from that of Recent *H. sapiens*. The cranial capacity (as inferred by comparative studies of modern skulls whose occipital and parietal bones show similar dimensions and curvatures) was probably about 1,325 cc. The basibregmatic height and maximum biparietal width are, indeed, rather greater than the means of the corresponding measurements of female British skulls. The inclination of the plane of the foramen magnum shows nothing exceptional. The occipital bone is rather unusually broad, but even this character falls within the range of variation of Recent European skulls. The endocranial cast provides evidence of a richly convoluted brain, differing in no observable manner from that of modern man. Two features only of the skull bones may be exceptional—their thickness (particularly in certain regions, such as the anteroinferior angle of the parietal bone and the cerebellar fossae of the occipital), and the excavation (in so young an individual) of the rostral surface of the basioccipital by a backward extension of the sphenoidal air sinus. It is doubtful whether these features exceed the range of variation in modern skulls. But even were this found to be the case, there would still be insufficient justification for a specific distinction of the Swanscombe remains from *H. sapiens*. They would appear to represent, rather, an early and somewhat primitive variety of this species. The facial region of the skull may have shown peculiarities, but it is reasonable to infer that if these had been of the extreme Neanderthal type they would certainly be reflected in the anatomy of the occipital and parietal bones. Morant has shown that *H. neanderthalensis* can be distinguished from *H. sapiens* by the metrical characters of the parietal and occipital bones alone. This, however, is not the case with the Swanscombe bones. The imprint of the sphenoidal air sinus on the basioccipital suggests an extensive development of the accessory nasal air-sinus system, and this, again, suggests that the supra-orbital ridges may have been relatively large. But there is nothing to indicate that they were more pronounced than the supra-orbital ridges of the Steinheim skull.

THE QUINZANO OCCIPITAL BONE

The Quinzano occipital bone was found in cave deposits near Verona in 1938. The main interest of this fragment lies in its close resemblance to the occipital bone of the Swanscombe skull, as shown in its thickness, great biasterionic width, and the considerable assymmetry of the venous grooves. It was found in a Pleistocene stratum which also yielded *Elephas trogontherii* and *Megaceros* and implements of an archaic Mousterian type, recalling in their technique the Clactonian and Levallosian cultures. This fossil bone has been described by Battaglia (6), who refers it to the Riss-Würm interglacial phase (at the latest)—that is, to approximately the same antiquity as the remains of the Ehringsdorf and Fontéchevade skulls.

THE FONTÉCHEVADE SKULLS

In 1947, portions of two skulls were found *in situ* by Mlle G. Henri-Martin at a depth of 2.60 meters in a cave at Fontéchevade in southern France. The stratum containing these remains lies below deposits of Mousterian date and is separated from the latter by a layer of stalagmite which had been undisturbed. It contained implements of the Tayacian type (Lower Paleolithic), and a warm-temperate fauna characterized by *Dicerorhinus merckii*, *Dama*, and *Testudo graeca*. The archeological and faunal data are consistent with an antiquity corresponding to the last interglacial (Riss-Würm) phase of the Ice Age. Finally, the fluorine test showed the skull bones to contain 0.4–0.5 per cent fluorine, as compared with a range of 0.5–0.9 per cent for mammalian bones of Tayacian date and 0.1 per cent or less for human and mammalian bones from the superimposed Aurignacian level. As in the case of the Swanscombe skull bones, therefore, the evidence for the antiquity of the Fontéchevade skulls seems to be well assured.

Vallois's study of the skull cap (Fontéchevade II) and the fragment of frontal bone (Fontéchevade I) makes it clear that there is here no demonstrable difference from *H. sapiens* (146). The position of the upper angle of the frontal air sinus in the skull cap and also the evidence of the frontal fragment of the other skull make it perfectly certain that there was no strongly developed supra-orbital torus. The temporal lines are poorly defined and placed at a relatively low level, the general dimensions of the calvaria are within the range of modern human skulls (though the biasterionic width is unusually great), and the cranial capacity is

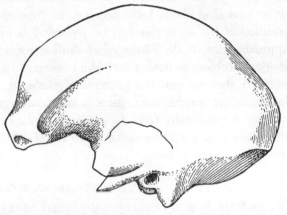

Fig. 6.—The Ehringsdorf skull. Approximately one-third natural size. (By courtesy of the Trustees of the British Museum.)

estimated to have been well above 1,400 cc. Apart from the biasterionic width, the skull bones are remarkable for their thickness, and in these two characters a rather striking resemblance is shown to the Swanscombe skull bones.

THE EHRINGSDORF SKULL

The Ehringsdorf skull (Fig. 6) was found in 1925 at a depth of 54 feet in travertine deposits near Weimar, in association with fossil remains of *Elephas antiquus, Dicerorhinus merckii, Bos,* and *Equus* and with fossil evidence of a temperate forest flora. The consensus of opinion assigns the skull to the latter half of the last interglacial period. The skull consists of the brain case only, and this has had to be reconstructed from a number of isolated fragments. However, there is little doubt that Weidenreich's reconstruction (151) gives a reasonably accurate representation of the calvaria (though it does not permit complete accuracy of measurement of over-all dimensions). The supra-orbital ridges are heavily built and in this respect (like those of the Steinheim skull) show some degree of approximation to the massive supra-orbital torus of *H. neanderthalensis*. On the other hand, the frontal region is filled out by a pronounced convexity to form a vertical forehead, the cranial vault is relatively high, and there is a well-developed pyramidal mastoid process. The cranial capacity has been estimated at about 1,450 cc., but, in view of the damaged condition of the skull, this can be regarded as only a very rough approximation. If the Ehringsdorf skull is considered as a morphological problem in itself (with the necessary qualification that the facial skeleton and the postcranial skeleton, if known, might lead to other conclusions), there is no valid argument for distinguishing it specifically from *H. sapiens*. It can certainly be stated that the calvaria approximates more closely to *H. sapiens* than does *H. neanderthalensis*.

THE MOUNT CARMEL SKELETONS

These important fossil specimens were found in caves on the slopes of Mount Carmel in Palestine, and they have been described in great detail by McCown and Keith (91). Those found in the Tabun cave were associated with a mammalian fauna suggestive of a fairly warm climate and (at a higher level) with fauna of a damper climate. The skeletons found in the other cave (Skhūl) were believed to be contemporaneous with some of the Tabun specimens. According to Zeuner (166), the Mount Carmel population thus extended through the last interglacial period into the first phase of the last (Würm) glaciation. The skulls all show a pronounced development of the supra-orbital ridges, but they display a remarkable variability in the degree of development of other features which are characteristic of the extreme Neanderthal type of later Mousterian times. In the rounded and vertical forehead and the height of the cranial vault, some approximate closely to *H. sapiens;* and this resemblance is enhanced by the rounded contour of the occiput, the strongly developed mastoid process, the smaller sphenoidal angle of the cranial base, the development of a distinct mental prominence on some of the mandibles, the moderate size of the facial skeleton (with a hollowing of the maxillary wall), and the slender, straight-shafted, limb bones. The striking variability of the Mount Carmel skeletons had led some authorities to suggest that they represent a mixed population derived from the interbreeding of *H. sapiens* and *H. neanderthalensis*. But this interpretation (which has no other evidence to suport it) has not been generally accepted. Indeed, recent studies by Higgs (52) and Brothwell (22) have now made it appear probable that the caves at Mount Carmel were occupied by a succession of different populations extending over a period of as much as ten thousand years—those at Tabun being of an earlier date than those at Skhūl. If this is the case, it is to be noted that the Tabun remains approximate more closely to the Neanderthal type while those from Skhūl show a general similarity to *Homo sapiens* of the Upper Paleolithic. It may be suggested, therefore, that the former were replaced by the latter in the shifting movements of populations in the Near East at this time. Taken in conjunction with the evidence presented by other examples of pre-Mousterian man, some of the Mount Carmel inhabitants appear to represent a transitional stage leading from pre-Mousterian *H. sapiens* to the later differentiation both of the definitive species *H. neanderthalensis* and of *H. sapiens* of a modern type. It is clearly a matter of some uncertainty how the Mount Carmel population should be placed taxonomically. However, since the morphological characters regarded as distinctive of *H. neanderthalensis* were evidently not completely stabilized in these populations, it is probably more appropriate to regard them as representative of early types of *Homo* not completely diversified specifically.

THE KRAPINA SKELETAL REMAINS

The Krapina skeletal remains were found in the floor of a rock shelter in northern Croatia, and the first results of their study were reported in 1901 by Gorjanovič-Kramberger (46). The basal strata (in which the human remains were found) are fluviatile, but the floor of the cave today is 25 meters above the level of the present river. In the same strata were found the remains of a warm interglacial fauna, including *Dicerorhinus merckii*. It is now generally agreed that the deposit belongs to the last inter-glacial period and is probably contemporary with the Ehrings-dorf site. The human remains are numerous but fragmentary; they include portions of several skulls, many teeth, and parts of the postcranial skeleton. All the adult skulls show a strong de-velopment of the supra-orbital ridges, and in a number of other features, such as the sloping forehead, powerful jaws, and small mastoid process, some of them approximate to Neanderthal man of later Mousterian date. On the other hand, the skulls show a considerable degree of variation, for in some the frontal region is closely similar to that of *H. sapiens,* and the skull vault is relative-ly high. The limb bones, also, are not distinguishable (as are those of *H. neanderthalensis*) from *H. sapiens.* The taxonomic position of the Krapina population is thus uncertain. It may pos-sibly (like the Tabun people) represent a transitional stage lead-ing to the final establishment of the specific distinctions found in *H. neanderthalensis,* the characters and the morphological features of the latter appearing only as irregular variations.

THE SACCOPASTORE SKULLS

The Saccopastore skulls were found (in 1929 and 1935) in a river deposit on the bank of a small tributary of the Tiber, at depths of 6 and 3 meters, respectively. In the same deposit were found remains of *Elephas antiquus* and *Hippopotamus,* and there can be little doubt that the human remains date back to the last interglacial period. The skulls show a strong development of the supra-orbital ridges, some degree of platycephaly, and a rather massive maxilla with reduced canine fossae. In these features it shows some of the characteristics of *H. neanderthalensis.* By con-trast, however, the cranial capacities are relatively low (*ca.* 1,200 and 1,300 cc.), the foramen magnum is advanced in position as in *H. sapiens,* the sphenoidal angle of the cranial base is small

(101°–105°), the occiput is well rounded, and the dental arcade is quite similar to that of modern man (with a marked reduction of the last molar tooth). Sergi (who has published detailed descriptions of the Saccopastore material) expresses the opinion that the remains represent an initial phase in a progressive development which later led to the specialized *H. neanderthalensis* (126, 127).

4. RÉSUMÉ OF THE RELATIONSHIPS OF *Homo neanderthalensis*

The problem of "Neanderthal man" has been the cause of much controversy for many years, and still continues to be. As already noted, the term was in the first instance applied to the remains of the later Mousterian population in Europe which was contemporary with the first part of the last glaciation of Pleistocene times and which, on morphological and biometric evidence, has been accepted by many authorities as a species, *H. neanderthalensis*, distinct from *H. sapiens.* Among the several distinctive features of the skull in this population is the enormous development of the supra-orbital ridges, which are united to form a continuous torus. When skulls of earlier date were later discovered, the term "Neanderthal" was also commonly applied to them, simply for the reason that they also display a strong development of the supra-orbital ridges. But, as we have seen, they do not consistently present the combination of other cranial and skeletal characters which have come to be regarded as forming a total morphological pattern distinctive of the species *H. neanderthalensis.* The taxonomy of the earlier remains has therefore been in some doubt. The clarification of the problem can only be finally made possible by the tabulation of the relative and absolute chronology of the Mousterian and pre-Mousterian remains and by a consideration of their morphological characters. Zeuner's study proved of considerable importance at the time it was published for the reason that he based his relative chronology entirely on the evidence provided by geological stratification, archeological data, and faunal associations, and without reference to the morphological characters of the remains themselves. Thus he avoided the bias of

75

some other students, who have allowed their assessment of relative antiquity to be influenced by preconceived notions that *H. neanderthalensis* was essentially a primitive type of Paleolithic man presumed to be directly antecedent to *H. sapiens.* On the other hand, Howell, making use of Zeuner's chronological tabulation, attempted to elucidate the relationships of the various fossil remains by making it clear that the later, or "classic Neanderthal," fossils almost certainly represent a peripheral development during isolation in the initial phases of the last glaciation. According to the view presented here, it is these alone which are entitled to provisional recognition as a separate species of *Homo*, i.e., *H. neanderthalensis.* Colloquially they may be referred to as the "extreme Neanderthals." While, as a matter of convenience, the earlier types which inhabited Europe during the last interglacial period may still be conventionally termed "generalized Neanderthals," it is important to recognize that morphologically they do not appear to be specifically distinct from *H. sapiens* (though there is some basis of argument for a subspecific differentiation). The major characteristics of the so-called "generalized Neanderthals" are the strong development of the supra-orbital ridges (to which, however, the Fontéchevade skulls are apparently an exception) and the great thickness of the cranial walls. However, in other features (so far as these can be determined in rather fragmentary specimens) they show a close resemblance to *H. sapiens* (Fig. 7).

It has to be admitted, of course, that the paleontological data regarding the origin and evolution of Paleolithic man are still scanty. But, on the basis of the morphological and chronological evidence at present available, the most reasonable (but still quite provisional) interpretation is that a primitive type of *H. sapiens* retaining strongly developed brow ridges came into existence by the Middle Pleistocene, presumably from an earlier small-brained type represented by the *Homo erectus* stage of hominid evolution; that *H. neanderthalensis* arose as an aberrant (and, in some respects, a retrogressive) collateral line from a pre-Mousterian or early Mousterian variety of *H. sapiens;* and that the former species eventually became extinct. Put in other words, it may be surmised that the progressive development of the brain in the *Homo erectus* group of hominids led eventually to the appearance of a type of *Homo* which, on morphological evidence, and in spite of the retention of some primitive characters of the skull, was apparently not specifically distinct from *H. sapiens*. At this point in the evolutionary history of *Homo*, two separate lines of development evidently made their appearance. In one of these the continued expansion of the brain was associated with a more

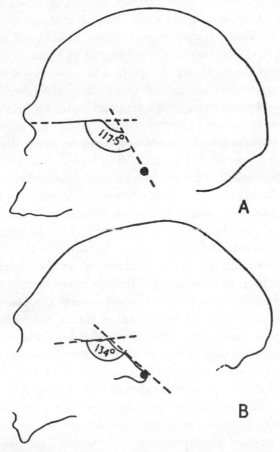

Fig. 7.—Mid-sagittal craniograms of (*A*) an early or generalized "Neanderthaloid" skull (Skhūl) and (*B*) a so-called "classic" Neanderthal (Monte Circeo), to illustrate the differences in the contours and the flexion of the basis cranii as shown by the sphenoidal angle. (After Clark Howell.)

exaggerated development of a supra-orbital torus and also of the jaws and palate, the appearance of certain specializations of the skull and teeth, and retrogressive changes in the limb skeleton, leading to the differentiation of a separate species, *H. neanderthalensis*. In the other line a progressive enlargement of the brain was associated with a recession of the supra-orbital ridges and the jaws, a diminution in the size of the teeth, the construction of a more evenly rounded cranium with a vertical forehead, and the retention of the limb characters already developed much earlier in *H. erectus*. This second line led to the modern races of *H. sapiens*. This interpretation, however, should not conceal the fact that the allocation of the remains of pre-Mousterian man of Acheulian date to *H. sapiens* is, in a sense, a taxonomic device which may or may not be substantiated by the future discovery of more complete remains. All that can be said at the moment is that there is no sound morphological reason for regarding the remains of Acheulian or pre-Mousterian man so far discovered in Europe as a species distinct from *H. sapiens*.

It is desirable to emphasize once more that the recognition of *H. neanderthalensis* as a separate species, distinct to this extent from *H. sapiens,* is still a matter for discussion. Indeed, in recent years there has been a growing tendency to include even the extreme Neanderthals of western Europe in the species *H. sapiens*. No doubt one of the main reasons for this changing viewpoint has been the assumption that the intermingling of individuals of different morphological types among the Mount Carmel people was the result of hybridization. But, as we have just seen, there is now evidence that the caves of Mount Carmel were occupied by different populations at different times over long intervals. The Krapina remains, and the discovery of skeletal remains of Neanderthaloid type at Shanidar in Iraq during the years 1953 to 1960 (137), also led to the conclusion that extreme Neanderthals and *H. sapiens* lived contemporaneously in the same region, with the implied assumption that they would have been likely to form interbreeding communities. But were they in fact sympatric populations? There remains some degree of uncertainty about this. Clearly, it is essential to determine with greater precision the time factor in order to decipher the late Pleistocene sequences with assurance. The last glaciation of the Ice Age, the Würm glaciation, was not a single episode of extreme cold; on the contrary, it was marked by a series of oscillations with intervening warmer periods (or interstadials, as they are called), and it is often difficult, on stratigraphical and faunal evidence, to determine whether a deposit containing fossilized human remains dates from the warm period of the last interglacial *preceding* the Würm glaciation or from the warm period of the first interstadial *following* the onset of the glaciation. It is here that the further application of the radioactive carbon method of absolute dating is likely to be of crucial importance. So far as the Shanidar skeletons are concerned, it can be said that on the information at present available they do show some differences from the extreme Neanderthals of western Europe, and, as we have suggested, the Krapina population (if all the individuals do comprise a contemporaneous population) may represent a transitional phase leading in one direction to specific distinctions characterizing *H. neanderthalensis*.

It seems certain, as Howell has pointed out (56), that the extreme Neanderthals of western Europe were evidently cut off as geographical isolates by glacial and periglacial regions for several thousands of years, so that they could have had little, if any, exchange of genes with hominid populations elsewhere. There would be nothing surprising in this, for it is well known that other mammals underwent speciation during isolation in the glacial and periglacial conditions of the Ice Age—for example the cave bear which is accepted as a separate species, *Ursus spelaeus*, the woolly rhinoceros, *Tichorhinus antiquitatis*, and the mammoth, *Elephas primigenius* (by some authorities regarded as sufficiently distinct to be placed in a separate subgenus of elephants, *Mammuthus*). If, as seems evident, these mammalian types, in adaptation to life in tundra and steppe, acquired a specific distinction from allied types, it is likely enough that *H. neanderthalensis* was an equivalent adaptation in hominid evolution—also specifically distinct in the degree of its divergence.

79

It has to be admitted, of course, that we do not know, and are not likely to know, whether the extreme Neanderthals were capable of interbreeding with *H. sapiens*. But even if they were, this would not necessarily negate a taxonomic distinction of specific status. The fact is that the category of species can only be defined in very broad terms, for example, in the phrase that "different species are usually not capable of interbreeding with each other, or in natural circumstances do not do so." It is well established that recognized species of lower Primates can, and do, interbreed, and even different genera may in some cases be interfertile. The recognition of *H. neanderthalensis* as a distinct species of the genus *Homo* can only be argued and accepted on the morphological evidence—that is to say, it can only be regarded as a "morphospecies"; the evidence for such a taxonomic determination rests primarily on the structural contrast with *H. sapiens* which the extreme Neanderthals show—a contrast which (as we have noted) appears to equate in degree with that shown by *H. erectus,* on the homogeneity which they display in such skeletal characters as have been studied statistically, on the fact that they differ more from any of the modern races of *H. sapiens* than the latter differ among themselves, on the evidence of a temporal succession leading to their differentiation from earlier generalized Neanderthal types more closely akin in morphological characters to modern *H. sapiens,* and on their abrupt disappearance after the first climax of the Würm glaciation leaving no very clear indication of the persistence of Neanderthal traits in the Aurignacian people that succeeded them in the later Paleolithic. Finally, it is to be emphasized that if the term "Neanderthal man" is to be applied to any Paleolithic type in which the brow ridges are strongly developed, but in which the morphological features of the skull and the skeleton otherwise conform closely to *H. sapiens,* then of course it is a legitimate corollary to infer that "Neanderthal man" was directly ancestral to *H. sapiens.* Clearly it is here a matter of definition and nomenclature, and unfortunately not all anthropologists provide the required definition on which their nomenclature is based.

5. "NEANDERTHALOID" REMAINS FROM
RHODESIA AND JAVA

In the preceding section we have presented the paleontological
evidence for the argument that *H. neanderthalensis* represents
the terminal product (now extinct) of a collateral development
of the genus *Homo*, which stemmed from earlier types taxonomically not distinguishable (on the material at present available)
from *H. sapiens*. Although this evidence cumulatively seems reasonably well assured, it is still too meager to permit of dogmatic
interpretations. Yet another element of uncertainty in the Neanderthal problem is added by the discovery of fossil "Neanderthaloid" skulls in Rhodesia and Java.

The Rhodesian fossils were found in 1921 in the course of
opencast mining of lead and zinc ores at Broken Hill in Northern
Rhodesia. They consist of a skull (almost complete except for the
mandible), a maxillary fragment, a sacrum, and portions of the
pelvis, humerus, femur, and tibia (108). The skull is of unusually
massive appearance and markedly platycephalic, with a very
strongly developed supra-orbital torus, retreating forehead, a
strong occipital torus, and a large inflated maxilla lacking a canine fossa. The palate is unusually large, having an area of 41
cm.^{2} (as compared with an average of about 25 cm.^{2} in modern
English skulls). In these characters the Rhodesian skull undoubtedly shows a close resemblance to *H. neanderthalensis*. Yet there
are certain differences, the significance of which is not easy to
assess. Morant (93) has shown that the skull can be clearly distinguished in a number of independent metrical characters, such
as the relative position of the maximal parietal breadth, the basal
and facial lengths, and the absence of a backward rotation of the
occipital bone; and in these characters it actually approaches
somewhat more nearly to *H. sapiens*. In yet other features it
shows a greater divergence from *H. sapiens*. In general, however,
Morant concludes that Rhodesian man and *H. neanderthalensis*—
in the limited number of purely metrical characters of the skull
which he used for comparison—appear to be more closely related
to each other than either is to *H. sapiens*. Von Bonin (10), also

81

as a result of metrical comparisons of the skull, inferred that Rhodesian man represents a phase of evolutionary development close to the common point of divergence of *H. neanderthalensis* and *H. sapiens;* but in coming to this conclusion he did not take into account the paleontological evidence indicating the evolutionary development of *H. neanderthalensis* in Europe from pre-Mousterian types which are not clearly distinguishable from *H. sapiens.*

The evidence of the type skull of Rhodesian man must now be considered in relation to the other remains found at Broken Hill. In the first place, the separate maxillary fragment (described by Wells, 123) is considerably smaller than the corresponding region of the type skull, the dimensions of the palate coming very close to the maximum dimensions recorded for that of the Australian aboriginal and African Negro. It also has a definite canine fossa, the modeling of this part of the maxilla "being essentially as in modern human skulls." Second, the pelvis,[12] sacrum, and limb bones are entirely similar to those of *H. sapiens* and show none of the features commonly regarded as characteristic of *H. neanderthalensis.* The question naturally arises whether the maxillary fragment and the portions of the postcranial skeleton were actually contemporaneous with the skull. However, recent studies by Oakley (101), based on a spectrographic analysis of the lead and zinc content of all the remains, have led him to conclude that "there is little reason for doubting that at least all the human bones recovered from the cave in 1921–22 form a contemporary group"; and their size and robustness are also consistent with the inference that they are all referable to the same type as the skull. The artifacts have been studied in detail by Clark (27), and this archeological evidence indicates an antiquity of Upper Pleistocene probably corresponding to the Proto-Stillbay phase of the South African Paleolithic period.

[12] In the original monograph on the Rhodesian remains (108) the os innominatum was held to be entirely anomalous in the form of its acetabular socket, and on the basis of this unusual feature a new genus, *Cyphanthropus,* was created. However, this conclusion was later shown to be the result of rather a remarkable error of interpretation (76).

A second skull, almost identical in contour and morphological details with the Rhodesian specimen, was found in 1953 at Hopefield near Saldanha Bay, ninety miles north of Cape Town (135). The site of the discovery contained stone instruments of the Chelles-Acheul Paleolithic culture. The associated remains of fossil mammals indicate an Upper Pleistocene period. Thus it appears that this type of early man was widely distributed in Africa at this time. A small fragment of the lower jaw found in association with the calvaria of "Saldanha man" closely resembles in shape and dimensions the corresponding part of the Heidelberg mandible (42).

The "Neanderthaloid" remains from Java were found at Ngandong in terrace deposits related to the River Solo (106). The geological and paleontological evidence suggests that they are of Upper Pleistocene date, the latter probably corresponding to the last glaciation (von Koenigswald, 68). The remains, discovered between 1931 and 1941, consist of eleven skulls (all lacking the facial skeleton) and two incomplete tibiae. A detailed and well-illustrated description of this material by Weidenreich (158) was published in 1951, but, owing to his sudden illness and death, this is not complete. The skulls show very interesting resemblances to the Rhodesian skull, with marked platycephaly, a powerful development of the supra-orbital tori, and unusually thick cranial walls (Fig. 8). Except for the cranial capacity (which ranges from 1,150 to 1,300 cc.), and certain unusual features of the foramen magnum (e.g., its length and the upward deflection of its posterior part), the skulls approximate quite closely to *H. neanderthalensis*. On the other hand, the two tibiae are slender and straight-shafted and appear to show no difference from the tibia of *H. sapiens*. It remains possible, however, that in their shape and dimensions they also fall within the range of variation of *H. neanderthalensis*. Here the lack of fossil data makes it impossible to arrive at any firm conclusion; the fact is that much more of the limb skeleton of the Ngandong population of Java and of later Mousterian man elsewhere is needed for a satisfactory comparative study. Oppenoorth (106), who first described the Ngandong skulls, allocated them to a new genus,

83

Javanthropus, but he later retracted this opinion and gave to them the name *H. soloensis.* In this he was followed by Weidenreich, though neither of them attempted to formulate a diagnosis of this new species. Probably it is wiser to leave the question of a specific distinction undecided for both the Rhodesian and the Javanese remains, and to refer to them colloquially for the present as "Rhodesian man" and "Solo man." Weidenreich took the view that Solo man was derived from *H. erectus,* and in his monograph he refers to a number of morphological resemblances with that species. Other authorities have regarded both Rhodesian and Solo man as slightly aberrant forms of *H. neanderthalensis,* which, on this interpretation, must have spread widely over the world. Yet another view, which certainly demands serious consideration,

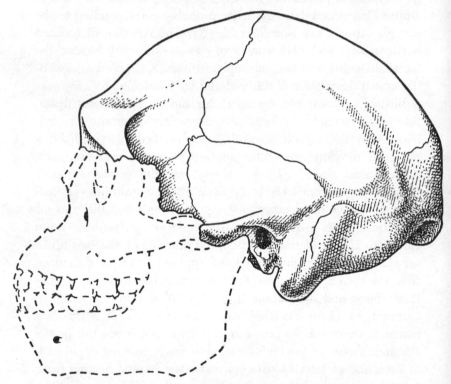

Fig. 8.—Lateral view of one of the Ngandong skulls, with a tentative reconstruction of the facial skeleton (after Weidenreich). One-half natural size.

is that these "Neanderthaloid" populations provided the basis for the independent evolutionary differentiation of some of the major races of present-day mankind, e.g., that the Ngandong population represents the ancestral stock from which the Australoid people were evolved and that Rhodesian man was the precursor of the modern Negroid races. The thesis of the polyphyletic origin of modern man, propounded from time to time by a few anthropologists in previous years, has more recently been revived by Coon in his somewhat argumentative enquiry into the origin of human races (31). This author relies for his evidence on remains (too scanty remains it would seem) of fossil man in China,[13] Java, Africa, and Europe, which for him suggest that the modern racial groups of Mongoloid, Australoid, Negroid (or Congoid), "Capoid," and Caucasoid peoples developed independently from a common ancestral species, *H. erectus*, several hundred thousand years ago. In other words, he proposes that *H. erectus* evolved into *H. sapiens* "not once but five times, as each subspecies, living in its own territory, passed a critical threshold from a more brutal to a more sapient state." Such a mode of evolution, i.e., a species A becoming differentiated into subspecies A^1, A^2, A^3, A^4, and A^5, and all these evolving independently to form subspecies B^1, B^2, B^3, B^4, and B^5, that together constitute a new species B, is a theoretical possibility, but it would be very difficult to demonstrate conclusively except where *complete* isolation of the subspecies and their several descendants is known to have occurred. Parallelism in evolution certainly does occur, but the probabilities decrease not only in proportion to the number of parallel lines postulated but also with the opportunities for a relatively free gene flow between descendant types. Since it is now well established that the species *H. sapiens* was in existence some 200,000 years ago, it appears highly probable that members of the species could have migrated many times during this prolonged period over wide distances of the Old World. Thus, while it may be that, for example, representatives of *H. erectus* in China did contribute at least some genes toward the composition of the Mongoloid

[13] For a recent review on "New evidence of fossil man in China," see Chang (26).

genotype, there is no reason to suppose that they did so exclusively. In order to substantiate so unlikely a thesis of the independent origin of modern human races as far back as the *H. erectus* phase of hominid evolution a much more complete fossil record would be necessary, and unless or until this becomes available it is reasonable to assume, as a matter of probabilities, that the several modern subspecies of mankind became differentiated after *H. sapiens* had in fact become established as a definitive species.

6. The Genus *Homo*

We have attempted to give a diagnosis of the species *H. sapiens* and *H. neanderthalensis* on the basis of skeletal characters, so as to provide some standard of comparison for further paleontological studies. For the same reason it is also desirable to provide a formal diagnosis of the genus *Homo*. The following provisional diagnosis is suggested:

A genus of the family Hominidae, distinguished mainly by a large cranial capacity with a mean value of more than 1,100 cc. but with a range of variation from about 900 cc. to almost 2,000 cc.; supra-orbital ridges variably developed, becoming secondarily much enlarged to form a massive torus in the species *H. erectus* and *H. neanderthalensis,* and showing considerable reduction in *H. sapiens;* facial skeleton orthognathous or moderately prognathous; occipital condyles situated approximately at the middle of the cranial length; temporal ridges variable in their height on the cranial wall, but never reaching the mid-line to form a sagittal crest; mental eminence well marked in *H. sapiens* but absent in *H. erectus* and feeble or absent in *H. neanderthalensis;* dental arcade evenly rounded, usually with no diastema; first lower premolar bicuspid with a much reduced lingual cusp; molar teeth rather variable in size, with a relative reduction of the last molar; canines relatively small, with no overlapping after the initial stages of wear, limb skeleton adapted for a fully erect posture and gait.

The geologic antiquity of the genus *Homo* is not certainly determinable on the fossil record at present available. It undoubtedly extends back to the first interglacial period, which, at a conservative estimate, was about 500,000 years ago. We have noted, also, that Swanscombe man, on the evidence of the three skull bones which have been found, does not appear to be specifically distinct from *H. sapiens,* and, with the necessary reservation that this conclusion may be falsified by the discovery of more complete remains, this carries the species back to the second interglacial period, which (again at a conservative estimate) was probably about 200,000 years ago. Another fossil to which reference should be made here is the mandible found in the Mauer sands near Heidelberg in 1908. On stratigraphic and faunal evidence this is assigned by most authorities to the first interglacial period, giving it an antiquity of more than 400,000 years. The type represented by this fossil is commonly referred to as *H. heidelbergensis,* but its taxonomic allocation must, in the absence of further evidence, remain uncertain. The mandible is of massive build and lacks a mental eminence. The dentition is entirely hominid in its morphological characters, and there can therefore be no doubt that the fossil is referable to the Hominidae. But whether it comes within our definition of the genus *Homo* can be determined only by the characters of the skull as a whole, which are at present unknown.[14]

[14] It would be inappropriate not to make some mention here of the famous Piltdown skull. For more than forty years this odd assemblage of relics, consisting of cranial fragments of essentially modern human appearance and a mandible and canine of simian form, has been the subject of speculation and controversy. Indeed, many authorities had been led to conclude that they present an insoluble problem. The solution of the Piltdown puzzle was at last achieved as the result of most intensive studies (initiated by the Department of Anatomy at Oxford University in collaboration with the Department of Geology at the British Museum) which demonstrated quite clearly that the mandible and canine tooth are those of a modern large ape which had been faked with the most remarkable skill to simulate fossilized material (159). The elimination of "Piltdown man" from further consideration greatly clarified discussions on the origin of man, for it has to be realized that, in both its curious combination of incongruous morphological features and its time sequence, it was entirely out of conformity with all the fossil evidence of hominid evolution available from other parts of the world. The exposure of this astonishing fraud is also important because it does serve to emphasize even more strongly the extreme caution which needs to be exercised in the interpretation of alleged fossils of a quite unusual or unexpected type.

CHAPTER III

Homo erectus

1. THE DISCOVERY OF Homo erectus IN JAVA

In the last chapter we briefly reviewed the evidence for the existence in Europe during the last interglacial period of pre-Mousterian hominids not clearly distinguishable as a separate species from *Homo sapiens*. We saw that the few skulls so far available from deposits of this date are mostly characterized by a rather heavy development of the supra-orbital ridges (closely comparable with those not uncommonly found in Australian aboriginals today); to this extent they certainly present a somewhat primitive appearance. We have also noted the evidence of the Swanscombe skull bones that the species *H. sapiens* may already have been in existence during the second interglacial period. We now have to consider a group of extinct hominids of much more primitive appearance, known from skulls, teeth, and limb bones found in the Far East and North Africa which have been for many years commonly regarded as representing a separate genus of the Hominidae, *Pithecanthropus*. Today there is a general consensus of opinion that they are more properly to be included in the genus *Homo*, but specifically distinct from *H. sapiens* and *H. neanderthalensis*. The generic term *Pithecanthropus* has thus now to be replaced by the specific denomination *Homo erectus*. The term *Pithecanthropus* has been time-honoured for almost seventy years, and it may be disconcerting to those familiar with it to accustom themselves to its replacement by the specific name *H. erectus*. But the morphological arguments for this change of nomenclature seem to be well-founded, and we shall now conform to it even though it may at first lead to some confusion for anthropologists long accustomed to *"Pithecanthropus."* We propose to ease this transitional period of nomenclatural change by using the colloquial term "pithecanthropines" here and there, and also by occasionally inserting the term *Pithecanthropus* in parentheses after the term *H. erectus.*

Homo erectus (*Pithecanthropus*) was for many years known only from two regions, Java (central and eastern) and China (Choukoutien, near Pekin). The Chinese fossils were at one time assigned to a distinct genus, *Sinanthropus,* but there is now general agreement that they are conspecific with the Javanese fossils. However, they present certain minor contrasts in skeletal and dental characters, which may be taken to indicate at least a subspecific difference.

The first outstanding discovery of *H. erectus* (*Pithecanthropus*) was made by Dubois at Trinil in central Java in 1891. The remains were recovered from alluvial deposits on the bank of the Solo River, at a stratigraphic level from which has also been derived a faunal assemblage including *Stegodon trigonocephalus, Hippopotamus antiquus,* a small axis deer (*Cervus lydekkeri*), and a small antelope (*Duboisia kroesenii*). It is now generally agreed that the Trinil fauna is post-Villafranchian, that the Trinil beds are of Middle Pleistocene age, and that they were probably laid down at a time corresponding to the second glaciation of the Ice Age in other parts of the world (95). On the basis of potassium-argon datings it has been estimated that Java was occupied by *H. erectus* over a considerable period from about 450,000 to 500,-000 years ago (70).

The most important item of Dubois's original discovery was a calvaria of *H. erectus,* which, in the very flattened frontal region, the powerfully developed supra-orbital ridges, the extreme platycephaly, and the low cranial capacity (estimated at about 900 cc.), presents a remarkably simian appearance. So much so, indeed, that some anatomists at first refused to recognize it as a hominid calvaria at all and supposed it to be the remains of a giant gibbon. In the same deposits and at the same stratigraphic level (but 15 meters upstream from the calvaria) Dubois found a complete femur, which, in its size and general confirmation, is quite similar to the femur of *H. sapiens.* Some doubt was natural-

89

ly expressed (mainly because of their apparent incongruity) whether the femur and calvaria belonged to the same individual and whether the femur was really indigenous to the Trinil deposits. However, the accumulation of evidence speaks so strongly for their natural association that this is now generally accepted. In the first place, there seems little doubt that the femur was actually found *in situ* in the Trinil beds (and, according to Hooijer, 54, the field notes kept by Dubois show that his excavations were carried out systematically and accurately). Second, it has been reported by Bergman and Karsten (7) that the fluorine content of the femur is equivalent to that of the calvaria and also of other representatives of the Trinil fauna, an observation which is in conformity with the geologic evidence that they were contemporaneous. Third, remains of five other femora of similar type in the Leiden Museum have been found among fossils collected from Trinil deposits (three of them were described by Dubois, 43, in 1932), and these also show a fluorine content which is compatible with a Middle Pleistocene date. Thus they confirm that at this early time there existed in Java hominids with a type of femur indistinguishable from that of *H. sapiens,* though all the cranial remains so far found emphasize the extraordinarily primitive characters of the skull and dentition. Finally, portions of seven femora of the pithecanthropines from Choukoutien show that in the Chinese representatives of this population a femur of modern human type was also associated with the same primitive features of the skull and dentition. The combination in *H. erectus* of limb bones of modern type with cranial and dental characters of a primitive type is worth emphasizing, for it illustrates an important principle of vertebrate evolution—that the progressive modification of the several somatic systems may (and frequently does) proceed at different rates. This principle is well recognized by paleontologists but appears occasionally to have misled anthropologists. Such differential rates of somatic evolution may lead to structural contrasts which give an appearance of incongruity, and they are liable to be regarded as "disharmonies" because they do not conform with the sort of correlations which studies confined to living species may lead one unconsciously to expect. The true affinities of such fossil forms may thus be overlooked and misinterpreted, simply because they do not exhibit the particular combination or assemblage of characters of which we have created a rather rigid mental image from our preoccupation with the comparative anatomy of living forms (the latter, in many cases, being but the relics of a much greater diversity in the past). Differential rates of somatic evolution obviously need to be taken into account in regard to the taxonomic relevance of characters which are selected for assessing the phylogenetic status of fossil types (see p. 28).

For many years after Dubois's original discoveries in Java over half a century ago, no further remains of *H. erectus* (*Pithecanthropus*) were found, in spite of the efforts of the Selenka expedition of 1907–8. Then, during the few years preceding World War II, further important discoveries were made by von Koenigswald (64, 65, 66, 67). With the exception of an immature skull found at Modjokerto in eastern Java, these new specimens come from Sangiran in central Java, about 50 km. from Trinil. They were derived from two horizons, one corresponding to the Trinil deposits and consisting of sandstones and conglomerates, and the other an underlying stratum of black clay, termed the "Djetis layer." The latter contains a faunal assemblage definitely older than that of the Trinil layer, characterized by *Epimachairodus zwierzyckii, Leptobos cosijni, Nestoritherium, Megacyon,* and *Cryptomastodon;* and by some authorities this has been taken to indicate an Early Pleistocene date. Beneath the Djetis horizon in Java is a still older formation, which contains remains of one of the first true elephants, *Archidiskodon planifrons;* and on the basis of faunal correlations this deposit is regarded as Villafranchian in age—that is, at the base of the Pleistocene. If this interpretation is correct, the Djetis horizon clearly does not represent the *earliest* Pleistocene.[1] Hooijer (54) has pointed out that there is some doubt regarding the provenance of certain of the *H. erectus* re-

[1] There appears still to be some disagreement regarding the stratigraphic level of the Plio-Pleistocene boundary in the Far East. Von Koenigswald regards the deposits underlying the Djetis layer as Pliocene, since they also contain a molluscan fauna which has been accepted as indicative of Pliocene age.

mains discovered by von Koenigswald, i.e., whether their stratigraphic position is referable to the Trinil or Djetis horizons, because not all were found *in situ*. However, it appears to be reasonably certain that at least some of them came from the Djetis beds and therefore that the antiquity of *H. erectus* in Java may have extended back to the Early Pleistocene.

The fossil relics of *H. erectus* (*Pithecanthropus*) so far available are listed below. Those derived from the Trinil horizon are as follows:

1. *H. erectus* I, calvaria and femur discovered by Dubois in 1891.

2. *H. erectus* II, found in 1937. A calvaria, more complete than the type specimen and including part of the basis cranii.

3. *H. erectus* III, found in 1938. The parietal portion of a calvaria of a young adult individual (with the sutures completely patent).

The specimens known, or assumed on indirect evidence, to have been derived from the Djetis horizon are the following:

4. *H. erectus* IV, found in 1939. This consists of the posterior half of a calvaria, including part of the basis cranii, and a maxilla and palate with an excellently preserved dentition (except the incisors). It should be noted that there are, in addition, two small maxillary fragments with canines (mentioned, but not yet described in detail, by von Koenigswald, 69).

5. *H. erectus* B, found in 1936. A mandibular fragment (somewhat eroded) including the symphysial region and containing P_4 tv M_3.

6. The Modjokerto immature skull, found in 1936.

7. The Sangiran mandibular fragment, found in 1939 with M_1 and M_2 in position.

8. The Sangiran mandibular fragment, found in 1941, with P_3 to M_1.

Besides the new specimens recorded in this list, which have been described by von Koenigswald and Weidenreich, there is a large number of isolated teeth from the Djetis layers of Sangiran which still await description. Mention should also be made of the tiny mandibular fragment found in 1890 by Dubois at Kedoeng

Broeboes near Trinil (an interesting specimen, but not highly informative), and three teeth also found by him at Trinil. These three teeth were assumed at one time to belong to *H. erectus* I, but this allocation is now regarded as quite uncertain. Two of them, upper molars, are in a poor state of preservation and are likely to be the teeth of an orang (this ape survived in Java up to the Middle Pleistocene), while the third tooth, a premolar, is certainly hominid (but its stratigraphic position is questionable).

The whole problem of *H. erectus* in Java has unfortunately been much confused by the multiplicity of the taxonomic terms which have been applied to the various remains. The immature skull found at Modjokerto in 1936 was originally named *H. modjokertensis*, though there was no reason to suppose that it was other than that of a young individual of *H. erectus*. Von Koenigswald was also led to apply the specific term *modjokertensis* to other remains of *H. erectus* found in the Djetis layers at Sangiran "for morphological and stratigraphical reasons." However, he did not define any morphological differences which might justify a formal diagnosis of this new species, and, by themselves, the stratigraphic reasons do not appear to be valid. For, while the stratigraphic evidence certainly demonstrates that the pithecanthropines existed in Java during long periods of the Early and Middle Pleistocene, it does not preclude the possibility (or even the probability) that during this time it was represented by a single species, *H. erectus*. It may be noted that *H. erectus* IV was given the specific name *robustus* by Weidenreich (157), again with no morphological justification. As already mentioned, only the back part of the skull and the maxilla of this specimen were found. The back part of the skull shows no distinctive features whereby it can be separated specifically from *H. erectus*, and there is no other material available with which the maxilla can be compared. Of the two mandibular fragments found at Sangiran in 1939 and 1941, the latter has been referred, because of its large size, to another genus altogether, *Meganthropus palaeojavanicus*. The former, though quite similar in its general size and proportions, was given a specific distinction partly because of the wrinkled character of the enamel on the molar teeth (which may, however, be no more than the expression of an individual variation) and partly, it seems, because the specimen is rather poorly preserved, so that certain details of the dental morphology are indeterminate. The generic separation of *"Meganthropus"* from *H. erectus* (*Pithecanthropus*) can hardly be justified on the basis of dental morphology; the two premolars and the first molar which have been preserved in the 1941 specimen conform in their total morphological pattern to a hominid dentition of the type found in the 1936 mandibular frag-

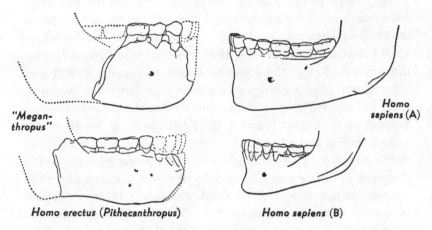

"Megan-
thropus"

Homo
sapiens (A)

Homo erectus (Pithecanthropus)

Homo sapiens (B)

Fig. 9.—The mandibles (reconstructed) of *"Meganthropus palaeojavanicus"* and *H. erectus* B, compared with two mandibles of *Homo sapiens* (an Australian aboriginal and a European), to indicate that the range of variation in the size of the Javanese fossils does not exceed that of a single species of *Homo*. Approximately one-half natural size.

ment (*H. erectus* B). The large size of the teeth and the preserved portion of the body of the mandible is certainly striking; but, as compared with the *H. erectus* B mandible, it does not indicate a range of variation exceeding that found (for example) in the single species *H. sapiens* (Fig. 9). It may readily be admitted that the available fossil material from Java is not yet adequate to decide finally whether there was more than one genus, or more than one species, of hominid living in Java during the Early Pleistocene. But from general considerations the probabilities seem to be against such a conclusion, and (it must be emphasized again) there is at present no really convincing morphological basis for the recognition of more than one species, *H. erectus*. In order to avoid further confusion, we shall here refer to all the specimens simply by the specific term *H. erectus*, while recognizing that there may well have been more than one subspecies or "race."[2]

2. THE MORPHOLOGICAL CHARACTERS OF THE JAVANESE
REPRESENTATIVES OF *Homo erectus*[3]

It has already been mentioned that the calvaria of the pithecanthropines in Java is known from four adult specimens and also one immature skull. Of the adult specimens, two are sufficiently complete to permit fairly close estimations of the cranial capacity by making endocranial casts and restoring the missing parts in proportion. According to Weidenreich, the cranial capacity of *H. erectus* I was probably not much greater than 900 cc., and that of *H. erectus* II is estimated at 775 cc. The capacity of *H. erectus* IV can be estimated only within rather broad limits, for, while the approximate breadth and height of the skull are directly ascertainable from the specimen itself, the total endocranial length has to be inferred indirectly from a reconstruction based on the other skulls. With these data, Weidenreich has calculated an endocranial volume of 880 cc. (or, say, approximately 900 cc.). Thus the mean cranial capacity of these three specimens is 860 cc.—a remarkably low figure when compared with the mean volume of 1,350 cc. for modern *H. sapiens*. The cranial capacity of the Modjokerto infant skull is estimated to be no more than 700 cc.; and, by reference to data concerning the brain growth of modern man and anthropoid apes, it may be inferred that this would not

2 It also remains possible, of course, that future discoveries will demonstrate that the owner of the *"Meganthropus"* mandible was so different from *H. erectus* in the morphological characters of skull, dentition, and limb bones as to justify a generic distinction. But the point is that, although I have a high regard for the judgment of my friend Professor von Koenigswald (which is, of course, based on quite considerable experience), I am not persuaded that such a distinction is valid on the fragmentary material so far available.

3 I wish to express my indebtedness to Professor von Koenigswald for his courtesy in permitting me to examine the hominid fossils from Java at his laboratory in Utrecht.

have expanded beyond about 1,000 cc. in the adult. So far as the meager fossil evidence goes, then, it may be surmised that the mean cranial capacity of the Javanese representatives of *H. erectus* was probably less than 1,000 cc.

As might be expected, a number of authorities have examined in detail the surface features of the endocranial casts of *H. erectus* in an attempt to find therefrom some clue to the intellectual status of these primitive hominids. Let it be said at once, however, that these studies have led to very disappointing results, for the information to be obtained from endocranial casts regarding brain functions is strictly limited. From time to time, indeed, dubious conclusions of this sort have been expressed, but they have mostly been based on a serious misconception of functional localization in the cerebral cortex and also on the false assumption that certain of the structural areas of the cortex (as defined microscopically) have rather constant relationships to sulci and convolutions. In the past, many inferences have been made regarding the acquisition of articulate speech, the degree of manual skill, the ability to learn from experience, and other mental faculties in fossil hominids; these must now be discounted. This applies equally to the assumption that right- or left-handedness can be inferred from a consideration of the asymmetry of the cerebral hemispheres (77). There is no doubt, also, that some previous authorities have seriously exaggerated the extent to which the fissural pattern of the brain can be delineated from endocranial casts. In lower mammals the convolutions of the brain are often outlined with great precision on such casts; but, unfortunately, in hominids and the large anthropoid apes the sulci usually do not impress themselves clearly on the endocranial aspect of the skull except near the frontal and occipital poles of the brain and in the lower temporal region (for a useful critique on the interpretation of endocranial casts, see Hirschler, 53). The most careful and critical studies which have been made of the endocranial casts of *H. erectus* are those of Ariëns Kappers and Bouman (59, 60), and a reference to their papers will show how cautious are their conclusions. In *H. erectus* I it is noted that the frontal operculum is not defined by secondary sulci, as it is in the majority of brains of *H. sapiens,* and the region of the frontal lobe below the middle frontal sulcus is relatively small. The sulcal pattern of the frontal lobe, in general, also shows rather interesting resemblances to that of the chimpanzee brain. So far as its general shape is concerned, Kappers finds that the endocranial cast compares most closely with *Hylobates* among the anthropoid apes (but, of course, it is very much larger and shows a much more complicated sulcal pattern). In the endocranial cast of *H. erectus* II, Kappers and Bouman found the sulcal pattern of the frontal lobe to correspond very closely with that of the other skull, and the conclusion is again stated that this pattern "shows far more affinities with that of chimpanzees than ever observed in man." It will be noted that the results of these studies are expressed entirely in morphological terms—and rightly so, for even the study of the gross anatomy of the normal human brain itself has so far not demonstrated any feature by which the intellectual abilities of the individual during life can be deduced. All that can be said of the brain of *H. erectus* is that the low average size is presumably related to a rather low level of general intelligence (cf. Fig. 12, p. 107). By relating cranial capacity to femur size, Brummelkamp (23) has tried to assess the degree of "cephalization" of fossil hominids. While the cephalization stage of less ancient fossil specimens of *Homo* (e.g., those found at La Chapelle-aux-Saints, Combe Capelle, Spy, Grimaldi, and Chancelade) is found not to differ from that of Recent *H. sapiens,* in the case of *H. erectus* (from both Java and China) it is lower by a factor of $1/\sqrt{2}$.

The main characteristics of the skull of the Javanese representatives of *H. erectus* may be stated briefly as follows (Figs. 10 and 16). The calvaria shows a very marked degree of platycephaly, with the maximum breadth low down in the temporal region. From this level the lateral walls of the cranium slope upward and medially to the position of the parietal eminence and then medially with a slight upward inclination to a median sagittal ridge. The supra-orbital torus is developed to an exaggerated degree and is bounded behind by a receding frontal contour and a very marked post-orbital constriction. The latter is associated with an inward curvature of the anterior part of the temporal squama, which accentuates the apelike appearance of the skull as a whole. The occipital torus is massive (particularly in *H. erectus* IV), and in all cases projects backward well beyond the level of the supra-occipital squama. The nuchál area of the occipital bone is relatively extensive (evidently for the attachment of a very powerful nuchal musculature) and slopes backward and upward to the

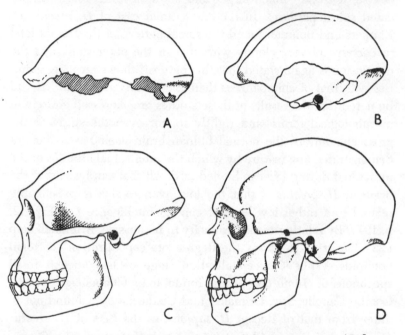

Fig. 10.—Comparison of the lateral views of the *Homo erectus* (*Pithecanthropus*) skulls found in Java with that of an Australian aboriginal. *A, H. erectus* I; *B, H. erectus* II; *C,* reconstruction of *H. erectus* IV (modified from Weidenreich); *D,* Australian aboriginal. Approximately one-quarter natural size.

occipital torus. The tympanic region and mandibular fossa are hominid in their general characters, but the rather weak development of the articular eminence in *H. erectus* IV and the rounded contour of the external auditory meatus in *H. erectus* II may be regarded as primitive characters of a somewhat simian type. The mastoid process is variably developed, and in *H. erectus* IV, where it is large, the apex is strongly deflected medially. The petrous bone, as seen from the endocranial aspect, is rather massive, and the cranial wall is everywhere of unusual thickness.[4] The foramen magnum (as far as can be judged from the crushed skull base in *H. erectus* IV) is situated as far forward in relation to the total cranial length as it is in *H. sapiens*.

The infant skull from Modjokerto shows features of particular interest. In age it may correspond to a modern child of about two years, for the specimen provides some evidence that the bregmatic fontanelle was just completing its closure, and the cranial walls are very thin (in the parietal region up to 3 mm., and elsewhere even less). The degree of ossification of the tympanic region, on the other hand, suggests an age corresponding to five or six in *H. sapiens*. But the precise age of this infant pithecanthropine is perhaps not a matter of great importance, for the primitive characters of the skull are in any case very obtrusive. The supra-orbital ridges are already assuming a marked prominence, with the incipient development of a postorbital constriction; the forehead already has a retreating contour; and the occipital region shows the development of the angulation characteristic of the adult pithecanthropine skull. If the individual were as old as six years, the small cranial capacity assumes a greater significance; if it were as young as two years, the strong development of the supra-orbital eminences, the retreating character of the forehead, and the advanced degree of ossification of the tympanic region become all the more remarkable.

The palate and part of the facial skeleton of *H. erectus* are known from specimen IV. The size of the palate is relatively enormous, the maximum maxillo-alveolar width, according to Weidenreich, being 94 mm. The maximum width, it should be noted, is at the level of the last molar teeth and may be compared with the maximum width, 80 mm., of the palate of the Rhodesian skull, which is at the level of the second molars. The facial aspect of this specimen shows a pronounced alveolar prognathism, a great breadth of the anterior nares (which is near the uppermost limit so far recorded for *H. sapiens*), and an extensive maxillary

---

[4] Even in the young adult, *H. erectus* III, the parietal bone reaches a thickness of 10 mm.

sinus. The lower margin of the nasal aperture is bounded by a simple margin, with no sulcus or fossa prenasalis. The 1936 Sangiran mandible, *H. erectus* B, is heavily constructed, with a very thick and sloping symphysial region, and there is no indication of a mental eminence. It shows three mental foramina—a very unusual feature in *Homo sapiens* but quite common in anthropoid apes. In its general build the mandible conforms quite well with the maxilla of *H. erectus* IV. The mandibular fragments found at Sangiran in 1939 and 1941 provide evidence of a lower jaw even more massive; but (as already noted) there seems no sound morphological reason for not including them in the species *H. erectus*. In both specimens the mental foramen is single and is situated about midway between the alveolar and lower margins of the mandible—a hominid feature which contrasts rather strongly with the low position of the foramen in the large anthropoid apes. In the 1941 mandibular fragment the symphysial region is exceedingly thick, but in its general contour in sagittal section it resembles the Heidelberg mandible quite closely, and in the high position of the foramen spinosum it also shows a hominid, rather than a pongid, feature. In none of these mandibular specimens found in Java is there any indication of a "simian shelf."[5]

That in its total morphological pattern the dentition of the *H. erectus* group of fossils from Java is characteristically hominid in type has not been a matter for dispute. The contours of the dental arcade, the shape, size, and morphological details of the canines and premolars, and the morphological details and mode of wear of the molars, taken together, provide a marked contrast with the pongid type of dentition. On the other hand, the few specimens available show certain primitive features, in which some approach is made to a simian level of evolutionary development. For example, in the specimen *H. erectus* IV, the upper canine, though not very large relative to the adjacent teeth, and spatulate rather than conical in general shape, projects well beyond the level of the premolars and shows a well-marked attrition

[5] This term is applied to the thin ledge of bone which, in the Recent large anthropoid apes, commonly extends back from the lower border of the symphysis across the anterior end of the interramal space of the mandible.

facet on its anterior margin, which indicates that it overlapped the lower canine to a slight degree. Moreover, it is separated from the socket for the lateral incisor by a distinct diastemic interval. Von Koenigswald noted that, of the two other maxillary fragments from the Djetis layers of Sangiran, one also shows evidence of a similar diastema, while in the other there is a contact facet on the canine which makes it clear that there was no diastema in this specimen. The primitive trait of a diastema in the upper dentition was thus not a consistent feature of the Javanese representatives of *H. erectus.* From isolated teeth (not hitherto described in detail), von Koenigswald (69) concluded that the central upper incisors are "extremely shovel-shaped, by far surpassing the condition observed in *Sinanthropus.*" The upper molars, premolars, and canine form converging rows on either side of the palate, with only a slight degree of curvature. The first upper premolars (two specimens) are provided with three roots, as is normally the case in the Pongidae but uncommonly in *H. sapiens.* The upper molars are large, the second molar being larger than the first.[6]

Of the lower dentition, the mandibular fragment *H. erectus* B shows in a fairly well-preserved state the second premolar and the three molar teeth. The latter are noteworthy for their large size and for the fact that their length increases progressively from front to back. This is a primitive feature only very rarely found in *H. sapiens* (four examples were found by De Terra, 142, in a series of 1,000 skulls). The alveolar socket for the first premolar is simple and indicates the single root construction characteristic of the Hominidae. The socket for the canine tooth is quite small (particularly when considered in relation to the massiveness of the jaw) and is placed medially to the anterior margin of the first premolar socket. Von Koenigswald has commented on the weak development of the incisors and canines when compared with the large size of the postcanine teeth, a character which is even more marked in the australopithecine material from South Africa (see

[6] It is of particular interest to note that the over-all dimensions of the first premolar and the first molar of the australopithecine maxilla found at Sterkfontein in 1936 (see p. 154) differ from those of *H. erectus* IV by less than 0.5 mm.

101

p. 156). No isolated lower canines or incisors from Java have so far been described in detail. In the large mandibular fragment (1941) from Sangiran (*"Meganthropus"*), the two premolars and the first molar are well preserved but are in a somewhat worn condition. The first premolar is of the hominid type, bicuspid with well-marked anterior and posterior foveae, and shows no tendency toward the sectorialization which is in general characteristic of Pongidae (fossil and Recent). There is a surface indication of a subdivision of the root, but no separation of the component elements. The socket for the canine shows that this tooth was surprisingly small, the total length of the root being certainly not more than 20 mm. Von Koenigswald (69) mentioned an isolated lower canine from Java, which he also referred to *"Meganthropus,"* but gave no details of this specimen except to say that it is small (presumably relative to the other teeth) and "in no way different from the canine of modern man except for the size." It should be noted that the preserved teeth in the large 1941 Sangiran mandible are quite similar to those of the *H. erectus* B mandible, except for their over-all dimensions. Weidenreich has also emphasized their strong resemblance to the corresponding teeth of the Pekin representatives of *H. erectus,* particularly in the arrangement of the cusps, the distinctness of the anterior and posterior foveae, and the development of the cingulum of the first premolar tooth. Some authorities have interpreted the large mandibular fragments from Sangiran as evidence for the existence in Java during the Pleistocene of "giant" hominids. This seems to be a misapplication of the term "giant," which is commonly taken to refer to stature. But a large hominid jaw does not imply a giant individual. On the contrary, so far as other paleontological evidence goes, there is some reason for assuming a negative correlation between the size of the mandible and the total stature. Certainly, in the case of the Javanese fossils, the femora, which can be assigned with reasonable certainty to the Trinil horizon, provide no evidence of great height—estimates based on these specimens indicate a stature of about 5 feet 8 inches or less, and in no case more than 5 feet 10 inches. It has already been noted that all these thigh bones (including the complete femur originally found by Dubois in 1891 and the incomplete shafts later discovered among other fossil material from Java) are quite similar to those of *H. sapiens;* if there is any minor difference of a biometric character, this has yet to be demonstrated.

If the calvariae of *H. erectus* (*Pithecanthropus*) are considered critically by themselves, it is perhaps not surprising that, at first sight, the original discovery gave rise to some doubt in the minds of anatomists whether it represented a primitive hominid or a giant gibbon. But the latter interpretation was clearly based on the assumption that the skull of a giant gibbon would be only an enlarged replica of the skull of the known gibbon, reproducing, that is to say, the same relative proportions and the same shape. In fact, however, our present knowledge of processes of allometric growth of the skull and brain in closely related species or genera would lead us to suppose that if a giant gibbon ever did exist, the proportions of the skull and cranial cavity would have differed even more markedly from the known gibbon than a large chimpanzee does from a pygmy chimpanzee. Indeed, the *H. erectus* calvaria provides an excellent illustration of the fallacies involved in the direct comparison of shape and relative dimensions (whether by visual comparison or biometric methods) without taking into account the factor of absolute size (see p. 35). It was, no doubt, the superficial impression of "gibbonoid" affinities in the calvaria which led some authorities to persuade themselves that similar evidence could be detected in certain morphological details of the femur. In fact, however, as already mentioned, it has not been demonstrated that the femur shows any significant difference from *H. sapiens.*

3. The Morphological Characters of the Chinese Representatives of *Homo erectus*

It was entirely due to the care and foresight of Professor von Koenigswald that the important discoveries of *H. erectus* (*Pithecanthropus*) which he made in Java shortly before the last war were preserved intact. On the eve of the Japanese invasion of Java, he distributed the valuable specimens among his friends of the local population, and when he himself was liberated from captivity with the final defeat of the Japanese, he was able to retrieve them intact. In the case of the remains of *H. erectus* found at Choukoutien near Pekin, the story was, unhappily, very different. At the end of the war no trace of the fossils could be found. It is generally supposed that they had been crated for dispatch to a safe area and that the ship on which they had been loaded was sunk in the early stages of the war. Fortunately, however, detailed and comprehensive descriptions had been published by Davidson Black (8) and Weidenreich (152, 153, 155, 156), richly and accurately illustrated by drawings, photographs, and radiographs, and casts of the earlier fossils described by Davidson Black are available for study.

There is no need to recount here in detail the history of the first discovery of *H. erectus* (*Pithecanthropus*) in Pekin, for the story has been well told elsewhere (see Elliot Smith, 44, and Keith, 62). A single lower molar tooth found in 1927 at Choukoutien led Davidson Black—at that time professor of anatomy at Pekin University Medical College—to create a new genus and species of the Hominidae, *Sinanthropus pekinensis*. This decision, based as it was on one tooth only, was met with some skepticism; but Black's inference that the tooth provided evidence for the existence in China during the Pleistocene of a primitive type of hominid showing certain simian characters displayed in a remarkable way his perspicacity as a comparative anatomist. For, two years later, in 1929, an uncrushed and almost complete calvaria of a very primitive type was found at the same site. Its similarity to *H. erectus* I of Java was very obvious from the first, and subsequent studies and further discoveries finally made it clear that the Javanese and Chinese fossils were not generically, or even specifically, distinct (von Koenigswald and Weidenreich, 55). The generic term *Sinanthropus* has therefore now been discarded. There are certain minor differences, however, and, as already mentioned, these are held by some authorities to justify a subspecific distinction.

The Chinese variety of *H. erectus* is known from fourteen calvariae (or fragments of calvariae), as well as portions of facial

bones, many teeth, and a few limb bones.[7] The main features of
the skull are as follows (Fig. 11). The cranial capacity (based on
Weidenreich's estimates from four calvariae) ranges from 850 to
1,300 cc., with a mean of 1,075 cc. So far as this limited material
goes, therefore, it appears to indicate that the mean cranial capacity may have been about 100 cc. greater than that of the Java
specimens, and at its upper levels the brain volume actually
comes well within the normal range of variation of *H. sapiens*. All

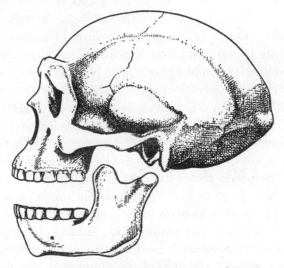

Fig. 11.—Skull and mandible of the Chinese variety of *Homo erectus* (formerly known as *Pithecanthropus pekinensis*), drawn from the cast of a reconstruction by Weidenreich. One-third natural size.

the calvarial specimens show a marked platycephaly, with heavily
constructed supra-orbital and occipital tori and a rather well-
marked sagittal ridge. They are relatively homogeneous in their
general shape but differ considerably in size (possibly an expression of sexual variation). Viewed from behind, they are broader
at the base, the width of the skull diminishing from the level of
the interauricular plane upward. Compared with *H. erectus* of
Java, the platycephaly is a little less extreme (though it should

[7] A complete list of all these remains (together with the sites of their discovery and the publications where they have been described) is to be found
in Weidenreich's monographs.

be emphasized that the cranial height can be only approximately estimated in the Javanese fossils), and there is a distinct, but slight, convexity of the frontal squama. The frontal sinus is unusually small in some of the specimens (in the Javanese types it is very large), though the other accessory air sinuses, e.g., in the maxilla and the mastoid process, are well developed. The bones of the skull wall are of massive thickness, the latter (according to Weidenreich) being due mainly to a thickening of the outer and inner tables. All the bones of the facial skeleton are likewise heavily constructed. The mandibular fossa is unusually deep, bounded in front by a conspicuous articular eminence. The tympanic plate is very thick and is disposed more horizontally than in *H. sapiens* (resembling in this respect *H. erectus* of Java, as well as the large anthropoid apes). The auditory aperture is wide; it varies in its shape but commonly has a transversely elliptical form. The mastoid process is relatively small. The nasal bones are said to exceed in width those of *H. sapiens,* and the nasal aperture (which is not bounded by a prenasal groove) is conspicuously broad. The palate shows the typical hominid contour and is not exceptionally large in its surface area. The cranial sutures appear to close earlier than they do in modern man. The mandible is robust, with a bicondylar width which reaches the upper limit of that of modern races such as the Eskimo (and perhaps exceeds it). The angle of inclination of the symphysial axis, according to Weidenreich, is about 60° and in this character corresponds with the Heidelberg mandible. There is no mental eminence. The digastric fossae (for the attachment of the digastric muscles to the back of the symphysial region of the jaw) are elongated and narrow and do not extend to the vertical inner surface of the mandible as in *H. sapiens.* The mental foramen is multiple in all the specimens found; indeed, there may be as many as five foramina—a remarkably simian feature. The ascending ramus is broad, and the muscular markings for the masseter and pterygoid muscles are strongly developed. The articular surface of the condyloid process shows no feature which differentiates it from that of other species of *Homo.* The coronoid process is broad and thick and presumably served to attach a rather powerful temporal muscle.

The endocranial cast has been studied by Davidson Black (9) and also by Shellshear and Elliot Smith (128). From the accounts of these authors it is very closely similar to that of the Javanese specimens of *H. erectus* and shows no real distinguishing features (Fig. 12).

The dentition has been studied in the greatest detail by Weidenreich (153) on the basis of 147 teeth found at Choukoutien,

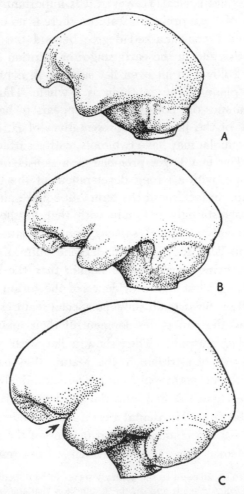

Fig. 12.—Lateral view of the endocranial casts of *A*, a male gorilla; *B, Homo erectus* (from Pekin); and *C, Homo sapiens* (the Sylvian notch is indicated by an arrow). One-third natural size.

107

representing probably 32 individuals. Of these specimens, 13 belong to the deciduous dentition. The teeth are large by modern standards, the enamel surface is frequently complicated by rather elaborate wrinkling, and the basal cingulum (i.e., the thickening of enamel at the base of the crown of the tooth) is particularly well developed. The canines show considerable variation in size, shape, and robustness, but those of the upper dentition are frequently large and conical. However, it is important to recognize that, in spite of these primitive features, there is no evidence that they projected to any marked degree beyond the level of the adjacent teeth,[8] and in the early stages of attrition they quickly became worn down to an even flat surface, in conformity with the occlusal plane of the dentition as a whole. Thus the upper and lower canines did not overlap, as appears to have been the case in some of the Javanese representatives of *H. erectus*. The first upper premolar may have two roots, with a surface indication of a third. The first lower premolar is a nonsectorial tooth of bicuspid shape, with a strong development of the lingual cusp. The two cusps, in fact, merit the term "subequal"; and herein the tooth contrasts strongly not only with that of the anthropoid apes but also with modern *H. sapiens*. For in the latter the lingual cusp seems to have secondarily undergone quite a considerable retrogression, being usually much smaller than the buccal cusp. The root is single but shows evidence of the fusion of two separate roots. The molar teeth show no special features, apart from their size and the strong development of their main cusps and some secondary cuspules. They show a flat wear with even a moderate degree of attrition; in this feature they contrast quite definitely with the anthropoid apes. The second lower molar is slightly larger than the first, and the third molar is usually the smallest of the three. The dental arcade shows the even curvature characteristic of the Hominidae, and in none of the specimens is there a diastema. There is some evidence from immature jaws

[8] Weidenreich's statement to the contrary seems to have been based on the comparison of *isolated* teeth and on the assumption that the base line of the enamel of the canine tooth is level with that of the adjacent teeth. This, however, is by no means the case.

that in the eruption of the permanent dentition the second molar appeared before the canine, a sequence which is characteristic of the anthropoid apes, but also of *H. neanderthalensis* and of certain modern races of man (e.g., Bantu). The deciduous dentition is distinguished by the fact that the first milk molar is rather strongly compressed from side to side and by the sharply pointed shape of the canine, which also has a well-developed cingulum. In both these features the deciduous dentition may be said to show a slight degree of morphological approximation to that of the Pongidae.

The limb bones found at Choukoutien comprise portions of seven femora, two humeri, a clavicle, and one of the carpal bones (os lunatum). It may be said at once that in no characters has it been satisfactorily demonstrated that any of these limb bones are distinguishable from those of *H. sapiens*. Indeed, it has even been suggested that they actually are the remains of representatives of *H. sapiens*, who, on this view, were living at Choukoutien contemporaneously with *H. erectus*. But this argument is based entirely on the a priori (and invalid) assumption that hominids with primitive characters of the skull and dentition should also show equally primitive characters in the limb skeleton; and it takes no account of the improbabilities of finding in the same deposits the skulls and teeth of one genus of hominids (and no limb bones), and the limb bones of another genus of hominids (with no skulls or teeth). Moreover, as we have already noted, the femora from the Trinil deposits of Java, which on a strong presumption must be assigned to *H. erectus*, are also of modern type.

Of the seven femoral remains found at Choukoutien, one consists of almost the entire diaphysis, one of the proximal half of the diaphysis, and the others are still more fragmentary (155). They show a marked degree of platymeria (though not more so than may occur in *H. sapiens*), and the wall of the shaft is unusually thick. Weidenreich expressed the opinion that in certain features of the curvature of the shaft the bones differ from those of modern man; but if such a difference does exist, it must be a very minor one, and it has not so far been demonstrated by metrical analysis. In any case, it could hardly be held to constitute by itself a very significant difference. On the other hand, the femoral shafts certainly lack the robustness and curvature characteristic of *H. neanderthalensis*. From the most complete shaft (femur IV), the total length of this bone has been estimated by Weidenreich to have been 407 mm.; and from this the total standing height of the individual is computed to have been 5 feet 1½ inches. If this were to be taken as representative of the local population as a whole (obviously, an unsafe assumption!), it would suggest that the Chinese population of *H. erectus* was shorter in stature than the Javanese population of the same species. The humeral fragments found at Choukoutien consist of a diaphysis of one bone and a small portion of the distal end of another one. Apart from the thickness of the shaft walls, they show no distinguishing features at all. The clavicle and the os lunatum are also quite similar to those of *H. sapiens*.

So far as the scanty fossil material permits a comparison of the Javanese and Chinese representatives of *H. erectus*, it is probably true to say that the former were more primitive in their smaller cranial capacity, more marked platycephaly, greater flattening of the frontal region of the skull, more heavily constructed mandible, less pronounced curvature of the dental arcade, larger palate, a tendency to slight overlapping of the canines with the occasional presence of a diastema in the upper dentition, and the relative length of the last lower molar. There is also evidence that in Java *H. erectus* extended back to a greater antiquity than in China, for while (as already noted) the faunal correlations of the Djetis deposits have been taken to indicate an Early Pleistocene horizon, the Choukoutien deposits are certainly no earlier than the Middle Pleistocene (corresponding, according to some authorities, to the second interglacial period and by others estimated on indirect evidence to be about 350,000 years old). On purely morphological criteria, however, the two groups appear to be quite closely related, the distinction being certainly no more than a subspecific one.

It is not known certainly what degree of cultural development had been attained by *H. erectus* in Java, for the evidence is

entirely negative. No implements were found in direct association with the skeletal remains. However, chopping tools, hand
axes, and primitive flake tools of the Patjitanian industry have
been recovered from deposits of a slightly later age, and it is not
improbable that such tools were actually made and used during
the Middle Pleistocene by hominids of the *H. erectus* type in Java.
At Choukoutien, in the same deposits yielding remains of *H.
erectus*, crude cores and trimmed flakes of quartz and silicified
rocks were found, forming a local industry of an archaic, but
fairly uniform, character. Animal bones were also found, broken
and chipped, apparently by design for use as tools. Finally, the
remains of hearths throughout the deposits, as well as charred
animal bones, provide evidence that these early hominids were
familiar with the art of making and using fire for domestic purposes, while the nature of their diet is indicated by collections
of deer bones and hackberry seeds. It appears, therefore, that, in
spite of the crudity of their stone and bone industry, the Middle
Pleistocene population of *H. erectus* in China had already developed a communal life of a very active kind; and it is of particular
interest that at this early time they had already acquired the
intelligence and skill to use fire for culinary purposes. Some
authorities have, indeed, expressed doubt whether the Choukoutien culture actually was developed by *H. erectus*, suggesting that
it was the product of a more advanced type of hominid assumed
to have been living contemporaneously in the same neighborhood.
But this suggestion has no factual evidence to support it, being
entirely based on the false supposition that hominids of such a
primitive morphological status as *H. erectus* would not be capable
of developing the Choukoutien culture. In fact, so far as the
archeological evidence can be assessed from the careful and detailed reports issued by those who excavated the sites at Choukoutien, the conclusion that the cultural and skeletal remains
were found in true association seems reasonably secure. It may
also be emphasized (as noted above) that, in spite of the low
average cranial capacity in some individuals, it came well within
the normal range of variation for modern *H. sapiens*. So far as
the volume of the brain is concerned, therefore, there is no

anatomical reason for supposing that *H. erectus* in Pekin was not capable of establishing a primitive culture.

Homo erectus IN AFRICA AND EUROPE

For fifty years or more it has been tacitly assumed that the primitive type of man now called *Homo erectus* (but, as we have already noted, until recently regarded as a separate genus of the Hominidae, *Pithecanthropus*) was confined in geographical distribution to the Far East. More lately, evidence has accrued to make it reasonably certain that the same type also existed at about the same time in Africa during the Chellean and Early Acheulian phases of Paleolithic culture, and probably in Europe also.

In 1954 there were discovered by Arambourg (1) at Ternifine in Algeria three mandibles and a parietal bone in deposits dating from early Paleolithic times—probably near the beginning of the second interglacial period. The jaws are remarkably robust and lack a chin eminence, the molar teeth are quite similar to those of *H. erectus* of Pekin, the canine teeth (as inferred from their sockets) were exceptionally strong, and the parietal bone conforms in size and curvature with known specimens of *H. erectus*. Indeed, there can be little doubt, so far as morphological evidence goes, that these remains do belong to the same species. It is unfortunate, therefore, that the group which they represent was at first designated *Atlanthropus mauritanicus*, with the implication that it was not only specifically but even generically distinct. This is but another example of the terminological confusion in paleoanthropology resulting from the misapplication of taxonomic principles. Other possible remains of *H. erectus* in North Africa are fragments of mandibles with the three molar teeth and one premolar tooth found in 1955 at Sidi Abd-er-Rahman in Morocco, but while the dimensions of the cheek teeth closely parallel those from Ternifine, the canine appears to have been more reduced. The antiquity of these jaw fragments is uncertain; by some authorities they are referred to the third glacial period and to the Acheulian phase of Paleolithic culture. The parts of a mandible and maxilla, together with a number of very

112

small pieces of a cranial vault, discovered as long ago as 1933 at Rabat in Morocco, have also been compared with *H. erectus* (145). But in this case the remains are too scanty to permit firm conclusions, and their allocation in time to the last (Würm) glaciation suggests that affinities with Neanderthal man are more likely.

Farther south in Africa, at Olduvai Gorge in Tanganyika, Leakey (74) has more recently reported the discovery of a calvaria from a stratigraphic horizon containing Chellean tools, and with an antiquity (based on potassium-argon dating) of 490,000 years (51). Thus it appears to have been more or less contemporaneous with the Javanese representatives of *H. erectus*. So far as can be inferred from a brief inspection of this important specimen and from published photographs (for it has yet to be described in full detail), the calvaria is so closely similar to some of the skulls of *H. erectus* from China that it would be difficult to justify a specific distinction. It is to be hoped that further and more complete remains of these ancient hominids in Africa will be found, for on the evidence so far available it certainly seems that *H. erectus* extended its distribution from the Far East to this continent almost half a million years ago.

The inference that *H. erectus* also occupied Europe depends (apart from the very indirect archeological evidence of stone cultures) on the interpretation of the mandible found at Mauer, near Heidelberg, and estimated on stratigraphical data to be about 400,000 years old. As already noted (p. 87), the taxonomic reference of this specimen must remain dubious until more complete remains come to light. Although the dentition shows certain differences, notably in their smaller size relative to that of the mandible, the massive construction of the latter, together with the conformation of the symphysial region and the vertical ramus of the jaw, recalls very closely some of the known specimens of *H. erectus*. The antiquity of the jaw, and its association with animal bones broken as if by design (like those found in deposits containing the remains of Pekin man), provide some further argument for allocating it to the species *Homo erectus*, but it still has to be admitted that such an allocation rests on very slender evidence.

A brief reference should be made here to some isolated teeth found several years ago among a collection of fossil bones and teeth from Chinese drug-stores (where such material was commonly sold for medicinal purposes). They were described by von Koenigswald and referred by him to a new genus of fossil apes, *Gigantopithecus*. He regarded this extinct giant ape as probably the latest survivor of an Asiatic stock which more or less parallels the human line, while Weidenreich took the view that it represents a giant hominid. Since then, three mandibles of the creature have been recovered from the Kwangsi province of China in deposits stated to be of Early Pleistocene date (26). The opinion is still expressed by some authorities that *Gigantopithecus* may be the product of a very early aberrant branch of the Hominidae. But, while recognizing that the molar teeth show certain morphological characters suggestive of affinities with the Hominidae, an inspection of photographs of the specimens (including a cast of one of them) inclines the present writer to the opinion that it was a giant pongid in which the dental specializations of the modern large apes were less strongly developed.

4. THE SPECIES *Homo erectus* AND ITS
RELATIONSHIP TO *Homo sapiens* AND
Homo neanderthalensis

The recognition of the species *H. erectus* has been based mainly on the skeletal remains of a number of individuals from Java and China, which, as we have seen, show a moderate degree of individual and geographic variation. But they comprise a group whose morphological characters are held by most anthropologists to be sufficiently consistent and distinctive to justify their separation as a distinct species of the genus *Homo*. If this is so, it is a matter of some importance (particularly for future reference in paleoanthropology) to provide at least a provisional diagnosis of the species, and the following formal definition is suggested.

Homo erectus—a species of the Hominidae characterized by a cranial capacity with a mean value of about 1,000 cc.; marked platycephaly, with little frontal convexity; massive supra-orbital tori; pronounced post-orbital constriction; opisthocranian coincident with the inion; vertex of skull marked by sagittal ridge; mastoid process variable, but usually small; thick cranial wall; tympanic plate thickened and tending toward a horizontal disposition; broad, flat nasal bones; heavily constructed mandible lacking a mental eminence; teeth large, with well-developed basal cingulum; canines sometimes projecting and slightly interlocking, with small diastema in upper dentition; first lower premolar bicuspid with subequal cusps; molars with well-differentiated cusps complicated by secondary wrinkling of the enamel; second upper molar may be larger than the first, and the third lower molar may exceed the second in length; limb bones not distinguishable from those of *H. sapiens.*

It will be noted from this definition that the distinction between *H. erectus* and *H. sapiens* is pronounced. Indeed, the cranial and dental differences (as well as the even more significant contrast in cranial capacity) appear to be almost as well marked as those which are commonly accepted as justifying a generic distinction between the gorilla and chimpanzee. The distinction between *H. erectus* and *H. neanderthalensis* is at first sight less obtrusive; but that it is a real distinction is made evident by the still greater difference in cranial capacity, the differences in the limb skeleton, and the more primitive features of the dentition in *H. erectus* (at least in the Javanese forms). It is made all the more evident by a consideration of the evolutionary history of *H. neanderthalensis,* which has led to the conclusion that the latter species was secondarily derived from a type of hominid more closely akin to *H. sapiens* and that its evolutionary development was associated with certain retrogressive changes in the skull. These cranial modifications show some resemblance to *H. erectus* (e.g., in the platycephaly and the strong development of the supra-orbital torus); but, in so far as they are retrogressive features, the resemblance is clearly not indicative of close phylogenetic relationship.

The relationships of *H. erectus* are obviously a matter of the greatest interest for the problem of the origin of our own species.

There is, indeed, a general consensus of opinion that *H. erectus* stands in an ancestral relationship to *H. sapiens* (and also *H. neanderthalensis*). This does not mean (as we have already emphasized) that the Far Eastern population of this species was itself the actual ancestral group—it means, at the most, that the species as a whole was probably ancestral to the later species; if so, of course, the transition from one to the other may have occurred in some other part of the world. The evidence for such a hypothesis is dependent on the following line of reasoning: (1) The morphological characters of *H. erectus* conform very well with theoretical postulates for an intermediate stage in the evolution of later species of *Homo* from still more archaic types approximating to the presumed common ancestral stock of the Pongidae and Hominidae. These theoretical postulates are based on comparative anatomical studies of the modern representatives of these two subdivisions of the Hominoidea and by analogy with the known evolutionary history of other mammalian groups. (2) The existence of *H. erectus* in the early part of the Pleistocene, antedating any of the well-authenticated fossil remains of *H. sapiens*, provides it with an antiquity which conforms well with the suggested ancestral relationship. (3) *H. erectus*, pre-Mousterian hominids such as that represented by the Steinheim skull, and modern types of *H. sapiens* of the late Paleolithic provide a temporal sequence which appears to illustrate a satisfactorily graded series of morphological changes leading from one type to the other. These arguments are precisely similar to those which have, for example, led to the conclusion that the genera *Merychippus* and *Pliohippus* were ancestral to *Equus*. But, whereas the fossil record of the Equidae has now accumulated in such detail that this phylogenetic sequence is as well demonstrated as any is ever likely to be on the evidence of paleontology, fossil hominid material is still scanty. Thus the inference that the species *H. erectus* was ancestral to *H. sapiens* must be accepted for the present as not very much more than a working hypothesis. But it is a working hypothesis which has the perfectly reasonable basis that it is consistent with the evidence so far available.

If the thesis is correct that the Hominidae and the Pongidae are divergent radiations from a common ancestral stock—the result, that is to say, of a phylogenetic dichotomy—the evolutionary precursors of *H. erectus* must presumably have shown morphological characters approximating much more nearly to a simian level of evolution. To some extent these characters might be tentatively predicated by a consideration of comparative anatomical data, by extrapolation backward of the *H. erectus–H. sapiens* sequence, and by analogy with the sort of morphological gradations which are known (from more complete fossil records) to have occurred in the evolution of other mammalian groups. For example, it is evident enough that one of the main features of hominid evolution (at least in its later stages) has been the progressive development of the brain; and there is some evidence that in the Early and Middle Pleistocene it proceeded with unusual rapidity in comparison with evolution rates in general (see Haldane, 49). It may be presumed, therefore, that in the immediate ancestor of the genus *Homo* the cranial capacity would certainly have been still smaller—perhaps, indeed, not very much greater than that of the largest anthropoid ape of today, the gorilla. With this would probably have been associated massive jaws and large teeth similar to those of *H. erectus,* but of somewhat more impressive proportions, and, in further correlation, powerful temporal and masseter muscles with extensive areas of bony attachment to the skull. Since the essential characteristic features of the hominid dentition (by which it is so strongly contrasted with the pongid type of dentition) were already well established in *H. erectus,* it might be expected that in the immediately ancestral genus these hominid features would also be clearly evident (in spite of the size of the teeth), though no doubt more primitive in certain details. Lastly, the fact that in *H. erectus* the limb bones had already fully achieved the morphology and proportions of *H. sapiens* strongly suggests that the evolutionary modifications of the limbs related to erect bipedalism had been acquired very early in the line of hominid development and would thus already be apparent in the ancestral genus. These inferences are, of course, based on indirect evidence and are capable of verification only by the discovery of actual fossil re-

mains. The remarkable fact is that they actually have been veri-
fied to a large extent by the discovery of the australopithecine
fossils in Africa (which are discussed in the next chapter).

A point of some importance emerges from the supposition that
the precursors of the genus *Homo* in the hominid line of evolution may have possessed a cranial capacity not much larger than
that of an anthropoid ape and were therefore, *in this particular
character,* not clearly distinguishable from an anthropoid ape.
As we have already noted (p. 10), the combined evidence of
comparative anatomy and paleontology makes it fairly evident
that the pongid and hominid radiations had become definitely
segregated for several millions of years before the expansion of
the brain in the Hominidae had become at all obtrusive. If this
is so, the taxonomic interpretation of the fossil remains of an early
hominoid with small cranial capacity—whether it is to be allocated to the Hominidae or whether it is to be grouped with the
Pongidae—will have to depend on the analysis of other morphological characters which may be accepted as diagnostic of the
evolutionary radiations to which the terms "Hominidae" and
"Pongidae" are properly applied. It is here, obviously, that some
attempt must be made to define the Hominidae, the more so
because different meanings attached to the terms "Hominidae"
and "hominid" by different authorities have quite evidently led
to much of the confusion of thought that is so commonly to be
found in discussions on human origins. Such a definition must
be based primarily on a consideration of the dominant evolutionary trends[9] which have characterized this taxonomic group (and

[9] It should perhaps be emphasized that the phrase "evolutionary trends"
is not meant to refer here to the *inherent* trends of evolution which have been
postulated by orthogeneticists. It refers to the graduated sequence of morphological changes which must obviously have occurred in phylogenetic history
to produce the known end-products of evolution and which in some cases
has been demonstrated (or at least partly confirmed) by paleontological evidence. Identical evolutionary trends in related groups imply a community
of origin, since they must depend on the possession of similar genetic consti-
tutions associated with similar potentialities for producing the same mutational
variations, and on these, again, depends the ability to achieve the same adaptations. In other words, identical evolutionary trends imply phylogenetic relationship and are to be taken into account in assessing the homogeneity of

which thereby serve to differentiate it from the evolutionary trends in opposite and contrasting directions which have characterized the Pongidae); and the formulation of these trends, again, must be based objectively on a consideration of the end-products of hominid evolution, as well as on the paleontological evidence so far available. For the paleontologist, also, the definition must be limited to those characters which are available for study in fossilized remains, i.e., the skull, skeleton, and dentition. The following definition of the Hominidae is suggested.

Family Hominidae—a subsidiary radiation of the Hominoidea distinguished from the Pongidae by the following evolutionary trends; progressive skeletal modifications in adaptation to erect bipedalism, shown particularly in a proportionate lengthening of the lower extremity, and changes in the proportions and morphological details of the pelvis, femur, and pedal skeleton related to mechanical requirements of erect posture and gait and to the muscular development associated therewith; preservation of well-developed pollex; ultimate loss of opposability of hallux; increasing flexion of basicranial axis associated with increasing cranial height; relative displacement forward of the occipital condyles; restriction of nuchal area of occipital squama, associated with low position of inion; consistent and early ontogenetic development of a pyramidal mastoid process; reduction of subnasal prognathism, with ultimate early disappearance (by fusion) of facial component of premaxilla; diminution of canines to a spatulate form, interlocking slightly or not at all and showing no pronounced sexual dimorphism; disappearance of diastemata; replacement of sectorial first lower premolars by biscuspid teeth

---

major taxonomic groups. It may be argued that two independent groups derived from a remote common ancestry might have followed identical evolutionary trends, leading to end-products not morphologically distinguishable. The answer to this argument is that, on the basis of the natural selection of random variations, the genetic probabilities are entirely against such a proposition, and in any case paleontology provides no evidence for extreme parallelism of this sort (see p. 17). So far as the Hominoidea are concerned, it is, of course, theoretically possible that this group may have given rise in the past to other evolutionary radiations besides the Pongidae and Hominidae. But, again, if this is so, no fossil evidence of any such radiation has yet been found.

(with later secondary reduction of lingual cusp); alteration in occlusal relationships, so that all the teeth tend to become worn down to a relatively flat even surface at an early stage of attrition; development of an evenly rounded dental arcade; marked tendency in later stages of evolution to a reduction in size of the molar teeth; progressive acceleration in the replacement of deciduous teeth in relation to the eruption of permanent molars; progressive "molarization" of first deciduous molar; marked and rapid expansion (in some of the terminal products of the hominid sequence of evolution) of the cranial capacity, associated with reduction in size of jaws and area of attachment of masticatory muscles and the development of a mental eminence.

It is to be noted that this provisional definition of the family Hominidae is not intended to be exhaustive, but merely representative of some of its main distinguishing features. It is also to be noted that all the characteristic evolutionary trends have not necessarily proceeded synchronously; as we have already emphasized, paleontological evidence of evolutionary sequences in general show that they not uncommonly proceed at different rates. But by an analysis of the total morphological pattern of a fossil hominoid (provided that sufficient data are available) it should be possible, even in relatively early stages of their initial segregation and divergence from one another, to determine whether such a fossil is representative of the evolutionary sequence already committed by incipient changes to the developmental trends characteristic of the Hominidae, or to those characteristic of the Pongidae.

For comparison with the Hominidae, the Pongidae may be defined in the following terms.

Family Pongidae—a subsidiary radiation of the Hominoidea distinguished from the Hominidae by the following evolutionary trends: progressive skeletal modifications in adaptation to arboreal brachiation, shown particularly in a proportionate lengthening of the upper extremity as a whole and of its different segments; acquisition of a strong opposable hallux and modification of morphological details of limb bones for increased mobility and for the muscular developments related to brachiation; tendency to relative reduction of pollex; pelvis retaining the main proportions characteristic of quadrupedal mammals; marked prognathism, with late retention of facial component of premaxilla and sloping symphysis; development (in larger species) of massive jaws associated with strong muscular ridges on the skull; nuchal area of the occiput becoming extensive, with relatively high position of the inion; occipital condyles retaining a backward position well behind the level of the auditory apertures; only a limited degree of flexion of basicranial axis associated with maintenance of low cranial height; cranial capacity showing no marked tendency to expansion; progressive hypertrophy of incisors with widening of symphysial region of mandible and ultimate formation of "simian shelf"; enlargement of strong conical canines interlocking in diastemata and showing distinct sexual dimorphism; accentuated sectorialization of first lower premolar with development of strong anterior root; postcanine teeth preserving a parallel or slightly forward divergent alignment in relatively straight rows; first deciduous molar retaining a predominantly unicuspid form; no acceleration in eruption of permanent canine.

Again it is to be noted that these evolutionary trends have not all proceeded at the same rate, nor have they all been realized to the same degree at the same stage of evolution. For example, there is now good evidence that in the Miocene the dental morphology characteristic of the Recent Pongidae had already been acquired (except for the hypertrophy of the incisors and the associated development of a "simian shelf" in the mandible); but the limb skeleton at that time still retained many primitive features suggesting quadrupedal locomotion of the cercopithecoid type (81, 86, 87). It seems probable, indeed, that the extreme specializations of the limbs for arboreal brachiation may have been a relatively late development in the evolution of the Pongidae. It has actually been argued that these Miocene hominoids are not to be regarded as pongids in the proper sense of the term, since they did not show some of the extreme specializations that are characteristic of the modern anthropoid apes. But this is to take much too narrow and static a view of taxonomic nomenclature (see p. 12). In so far as the term "Pongidae" refers to the subsidiary radiation of the Hominoidea which culminated in the development of the modern anthropoid apes, it must include all those types representative of the earlier phases of pongid evolution after this group had become definitely segregated from the Cercopithecoidea. Studies of comparative anatomy make it certain that the ancestral stock from which the modern anthropoid apes arose must have shown just such a combination of characters of an intermediate kind as those found in the Miocene hominoids; and a critical examination of the latter also makes it clear that they had already become definitely segregated from the Cercopithecoidea and that most of the known types were committed (so to speak) to the evolutionary trends characteristic of the Pongidae.

CHAPTER IV

Australopithecus

1. THE PROVENANCE OF THE AUSTRALOPITHECINE FOSSILS

In 1925 Professor R. A. Dart (33), of the Witwatersrand University in Johannesburg, described the well-known Taung[1] skull from Bechuanaland as representing a new type of hominoid, to which he gave the generic name *Australopithecus*.[2] He pointed out that, in spite of the obviously apelike proportions of the brain case, the relatively large jaws, and the pronounced prognathism, there are certain features (particularly in the dentition) in which this fossil hominoid approximates more closely to the Hominidae than any of the known anthropoid apes do. In general, other anatomists agreed that this certainly was so, but some regarded the morphological resemblances as little more than interesting examples of parallelism having no particular reference to hominid evolution. In 1936 and the following years, the late Dr. Robert Broom (at that time working at the Transvaal Museum, Pretoria) discovered at three sites near Johannesburg (Sterkfontein, Kromdraai, and Swartkrans) much more numerous and complete remains of similar hominoids, comprising many skulls, several jaws, parts of the limb skeleton (including two well-preserved specimens of the os innominatum), and several hundred teeth. In these excavations and in the study of the fossil material he was assisted by Dr. J. T. Robinson. Broom died in 1951 at the age

---

[1] This place-name has usually been spelt "Taungs," but it now appears that the terminal *s* has been added in error.

[2] *Australopithecus* means "the southern ape" and refers to the fact that this fossil hominoid lived in the Southern Hemisphere. The term has been criticized on etymological grounds. But its main disadvantage is that it is liable to convey to the reader of popular expositions the suggestion of a connection with Australia and also that (as it has now turned out) the creature is certainly not an anthropoid ape in the taxonomic sense.

of eighty-four; and since then Dr. Robinson was for several years responsible for continuing the excavations and for making still further important discoveries. At another site altogether, in cave deposits at Makapansgat (about 150 miles north of Johannesburg), Dart found, in 1947 and later, more remains of *Australopithecus,* including a crushed skull, an immature mandible, an occiput, parts of two pelves, and a maxillary fragment. It is apparent, therefore, that the Australopithecinae were widespread in the Transvaal.

With his collaborators, Broom described his remarkable collection of fossils in a number of separate papers and in three monographs (19, 20, 21). The material now available is so abundant that it will certainly take several years before anything like an exhaustive account of it can be completed. Broom himself well recognized this, and in his monographs published by the Transvaal Museum he attempted little more than to provide a general survey of his discoveries, illustrated by photographs and drawings. But his descriptions made it very evident that Dart's first appraisal of the Taung skull was basically correct—that is, that, morphologically, *Australopithecus* approximates to the Hominidae much more closely than any of the known anthropoid apes do (whether Recent or extinct) and that the genus as a whole may well include the ancestral stock from which *Homo* was derived (or that, at the least, it was very closely related to the ancestral stock). This conclusion was later reinforced by a detailed and careful study of the australopithecine dentition by Robinson (118). The history of these discoveries in South Africa has already been recounted more than once, and there is thus no need (except incidentally) to repeat it again here. All the australopithecine remains from the Transvaal have been derived from cave deposits or fissures in formations of dolomitic limestone and in most cases were firmly imbedded in a dense stalagmitic matrix. In the Olduvai Gorge in Tanganyika remains of similar or very closely related types have been exposed in well-stratified deposits considerably older than the South African sites. The South African deposits are mostly in the form of a breccia in which stratification is either absent or too poorly defined to permit, with any degree of assurance, a relative geologic dating on this basis. Estimates of antiquity, therefore, were at first based almost entirely on the associated fauna. Here, however, a real difficulty presents itself, for the faunal correlations of the South African Tertiary and Quaternary periods have still to be worked out in adequate detail. Many of the mammalian remains found in the australopithecine deposits belong to extinct forms (e.g., *Machairodus, Griquatherium, Lycyaena, Hyaenictis, Dinopithecus, Notochoerus,* and a chalichothere). On the basis of some of these fossils, e.g., *Lycyaena,* which in Europe is representative of a mid-Pliocene age, it had been argued that the antiquity of *Australopithecus* in South Africa extended back into the Pliocene. But it is well known that a number of mammals which became extinct in Europe before the beginning of the Pleistocene actually survived to a much later date in South Africa, and this may have been the case with such types as *Lycyaena.* As Cooke (30) has put it: "It seems that this southern tip of the African continent was in the nature of a cul-de-sac in which archaic forms survived long after they had become extinct in the more rigorous and variable climate of Quaternary Europe." The fact that remains of *Equus* have been recovered from some of the deposits certainly indicates that the latter are Pleistocene, though there appears some doubt whether these remains were in all cases derived from exactly the same geological horizon as *Australopithecus.* There now seems to be general agreement that all the australopithecine deposits in South Africa are not very widely separated in geological time, and it is also probably fair to say that most geologists and paleontologists who have studied the evidence on the spot accept a dating of Villafranchian at the earliest—that is to say, the early part of the Lower Pleistocene. Apart from the indications which they may provide of geologic age, some of the mammalian remains in the australopithecine deposits provide very important ancillary evidence of the climatic environment at the time, for they confirm the geologic evidence that it was not very different from the present time, that is to say, a climate tending to aridity—it certainly was not a region of tropical forest, such as is suitable for arboreal anthropoid apes as we know them today.

This conclusion has received strong support from the analysis of the breccias and their sand content of chert and quartz at different sites (12).

Studies by Oakley (104), which led to a considerable clarification of the chronology of the australopithecine sites, may be briefly summarized as follows. The Sterkfontein and Makapansgat deposits appear to be approximately contemporaneous with the Taung breccia in which the original skull was found, and they may all be referred provisionally to the second half of the African pluvial period called the "Kageran" (which corresponds to the latter part of the Villafranchian). The Australopithecinae found at these sites were thus living at a time when the climate was becoming increasingly arid. The Kromdraai and Swartkrans deposits, on the other hand, were probably laid down at the beginning of the suceeding Kamasian pluvial period—a period of decreasing aridity. If this dating is correct, it means that the Australopithecinae were still living in South Africa at a time when tool-making hominids had already reached the Transvaal, for pebble-tools have been found in gravels that were evidently laid down before the end of the Kageran period. Implements of this type, the Oldowan industry as it is called, have actually been found in deposits at several different sites containing the remains of *Australopithecus*. It is a fair inference, therefore, that the australopithecines were themselves responsible for making and using the tools. Of prime importance in this connection was the discovery in 1959 of an almost complete australopithecine skull at Olduvai in Tanganyika, for according to Leakey (72) it lay on a "living floor" on which were also found not only Oldowan tools of material foreign to the site but waste flakes struck off in their manufacture, as well as many animal bones that had apparently been deliberately broken for the preparation of food. In spite of this association in independent and widely separated areas of australopithecine remains and fabricated implements, some authorities still hesitate to accept the obvious conclusion that the australopithecines were the actual fabricators, partly (it seems) because they find it difficult to suppose that creatures with such small brains would have been capable of making tools.

They postulate the contemporaneous existence of more advanced and larger-brained hominids who were responsible for making the tools and even of preying on the australopithecines. But it has to be admitted that no remains of really large-brained hominids have yet been found in the australopithecine deposits, and, in any case, the Oldowan implements are of such simple and crude construction that they might well be the products of small-brained hominids.

The establishment of the precise chronology of the australopithecine deposits is clearly a matter of considerable importance, and the Makapan Valley and the stratified deposits of the Olduvai Gorge offer the most favorable prospects for gaining this information. The Makapan Valley contains a number of caves with deposits ranging from the Kageran period to the Middle Stone Age of South Africa, and it may be possible to define a chronological series linking up the deposits in this area from which australopithecine remains were derived with those containing known sequences of Paleolithic industries. In the beds of the Olduvai Gorge the deposit containing the australopithecine skull (Bed I) underlies the level (Bed II) that has yielded large numbers of stone implements of an advanced Chellean culture, associated with a skull cap assignable to *Homo erectus* (see p. 113).

2. THE NOMENCLATURE OF THE AUSTRALOPITHECINE FOSSILS

The species represented by the Taung skull was named *Australopithecus africanus*. Subsequent discoveries by Broom led him to postulate three other genera—*Telanthropus, Plesianthropus,* and *Paranthropus*—and to divide the last into two species, *P. robustus* and *P. crassidens*.[3] Lastly, the fossil australopithecine skull from Olduvai has been allocated to still another genus, *Zinjanthropus,* although it appears to be quite similar to Broom's *"Paranthropus"* (certainly no distinguishing features of a generic character have been demonstrated). The mandible found at a somewhat lower level in the Olduvai Gorge has been provision-

[3] According to Broom's classification, *Plesianthropus* occurs at the Sterkfontein site, *Australopithecus* at Taung, *Paranthropus robustus* at Kromdraai, and *P. crassidens* and *Telanthropus* at Swartkrans.

ally labelled by Leakey (74) *"pre-Zinjanthropus,"* but the dentition appears to conform with the Sterkfontein specimens of *Australopithecus,* particularly in the characteristic shape of the
canine tooth. The multiplication of taxonomic terms undoubtedly tended to sidetrack the main issues in the controversies which
followed the first announcements of the discoveries, and it was
probably also responsible for some degree of the skepticism at
first expressed by certain anatomists in regard to them. Broom
thought he was able to detect morphological differences which
justified the recognition of four different genera, and he believed
this was further supported by paleontological evidence of a considerable gap in geologic time separating one genus from another.
However, as we have noted, the consensus of opinion among
geologists who have examined the sites is that they are, broadly
speaking, closely contemporaneous or that, in any case, the time
sequences are not so different as to justify generic distinctions
which have only a doubtful morphological basis. But the main
point of criticism is that at the time of their discovery none of the
several genera and species was adequately defined in formal
diagnoses, nor has it yet been really satisfactorily demonstrated
that the morphological differences are in fact greater than may be
explained by individual or sexual variation or by variations in
local races or geographical varieties of the same species. Such
differences as do exist may justify subspecific distinctions or possibly even specific distinctions. But it appears certain that, at the
most, they are no greater than those which (for example) distinguish the two closely related species of chimpanzee, *Pan
satyrus* and *P. paniscus.* Further, if, as it is now generally agreed,
the morphological contrasts between *Homo erectus* (i.e., *Pithecanthropus* of a previous nomenclature) and *Homo sapiens* are
not sufficiently obtrusive to permit of more than a specific distinction from the latter, then by comparison it would be difficult to
justify more than a specific distinction for the australopithecines
from different localities. The crucial argument for a taxonomic
differentiation among the South and East African fossil australopithecines must ultimately depend on (1) the demonstration of
the range of variation which each local group shows and (2) how

128

far the variations compare with those which are accepted as adequate for specific or generic distinctions in other related groups of hominoids (i.e., in the Hominidae and Pongidae). In agreement with Washburn and Patterson (149), the view taken here, at least provisionally, is that all the australopithecine remains so far discovered represent one genus only, *Australopithecus,* but that they may represent more than one species. In order to avoid confusion, they will collectively be referred to as the Australopithecinae (or more colloquially, the australopithecines), even though it may eventually be decided that to place them in a separate subfamily is carrying their taxonomic distinction too far. So far as the different local groups of the Australopithecinae are concerned, it seems better, for the present, to avoid the different generic and specific terms which have been applied by their discoverers (apart from *Australopithecus*) and to use the place-names of the local sites for reference purposes. Thus we may refer to the Kromdraai skull (instead of the skull of *Paranthropus*), the Sterkfontein pelvis (instead of the pelvis of *Plesianthropus*), or the Olduvai australopithecines.[4]

3. THE MORPHOLOGICAL CHARACTERS OF THE AUSTRALOPITHECINAE[5]

The cranial, skeletal, and dental morphology of the Australopithecinae is now known from fossil material notable for its great

---

[4] Recent suggestions that *"Telanthropus"* is synonymous with *Homo erectus,* and that *"pre-Zinjanthropus"* is to be accepted as a very early representative of the genus *Homo,* specifically named *"Homo habilis,"* may be discounted. An examination by the present author of some of the original specimens and of excellent casts of others has led him seriously to doubt the validity of these taxonomic labels, for the latter take no account of presumptive individual, geographical, or temporal variability in the australopithecines. In this connection reference should be made to a recent and most timely publication by A. H. Schultz on "Age Changes, Sex Differences, and Variability as Factors in the Classification of the Primates," in *Classification and Human Evolution* (Chicago: Aldine Publ. Co., 1963), p. 85.

[5] I wish to express my indebtedness to Professor Raymond Dart and the late Dr. Robert Broom for all the facilities which they provided in order to allow me to study the fossil material in their care in 1947 and also to visit the sites where they were discovered. I am also most grateful to Dr. J. T. Robinson for giving me the opportunity of examining some of the more recently discovered fossils.

quantity and for the completeness and excellent state of preservation of many of the specimens. Indeed, it is probably true to say that we now know a good deal more about the anatomy of this group and its range of morphological variation than of any other group of fossil hominoids.

THE SKULL AND ENDOCRANIAL CAST

Skulls and mandibles (or portions of them) representing juveniles, adolescents, and adults young and old have been found at the sites of Taung, Sterkfontein, Kromdraai, Swartkrans, Makapansgat, and Olduvai. The first almost perfect specimen of a skull was exposed at Sterkfontein in 1947 (Sterkfontein skull V)— a practically complete and undistorted skull, from which, however, the mandible was missing (Fig. 13). It was found imbedded in a dense stalagmitic matrix and was developed therefrom with consummate skill by Broom (20). Almost complete, but severely crushed, skulls have also been found at Swartkrans. The Taung specimen consists of the facial part of a juvenile skull, almost complete and undistorted, associated with a natural endocranial cast. Still other skull relics are represented by portions of the cranium and facial skeleton from most of the sites in the Transvaal, numerous specimens of the maxilla and palate, and several mandibles. Some of this other material is rather fragmentary, but nevertheless provides information of critical importance. The australopithecine skull (*"Zinjanthropus"*) from Olduvai is that of an adolescent individual and is virtually complete (except for the mandible) (see Fig. 14).

The most obvious feature of the australopithecine skull as a whole is the combination of a small brain case with large jaws, and it is this which gives to it such a simian appearance. It is well to emphasize these simian proportions from the outset, because (as well recognized by Dart, Broom, and others) they are primitive characters in which the Australopithecinae contrast very strongly with *H. sapiens* or even *H. erectus*. But it is also important to note that, while the general proportions are certainly "simian" in the sense that they approximate to the level of development still preserved by the modern anthropoid apes, they

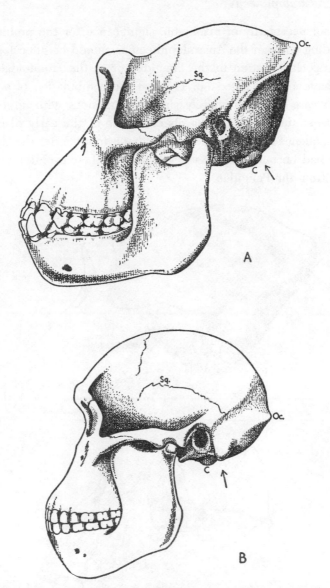

Fig. 13.—The skull of *A*, a female gorilla, compared with *B*, the Sterkfontein australopithecine skull No. 5, illustrating the more lightly built type of *Australopithecus* (*A. africanus*). In the latter the mandible and dentition have been reconstructed by reference to numerous other specimens. Note the relative position of the occipital protuberance (*Oc.*), the occipital condyle (*C*), and the squamous suture (*Sq.*). The arrow indicates the axis of the foramen magnum. Approximately one-third natural size.

are not necessarily of taxonomic significance for the problem of deciding whether the Australopithecinae should be allocated in a natural classification to the Pongidae or to the Hominidae. For we have already noted (p. 11) that the combination of a small brain case of approximately simian dimensions with large jaws must certainly have been a characteristic of the early phases in the sequence of hominid evolution, that is to say, after the Hominidae had become definitely segregated in their evolutionary history from the Pongidae.

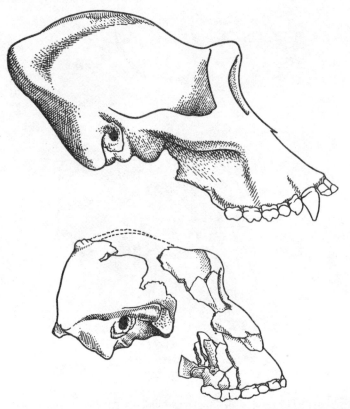

FIG. 14.—Side view of the skull of a male gorilla (*A*) and the australopithecine skull ("*Zinjanthropus*") from Olduvai (*B*), illustrating the more heavily built type of *Australopithecus* (*A. robustus*). Approximately one-third natural size. The orientation of the front part in relation to the back part of the australopithecine skull is slightly conjectural. (From a photograph by Dr. L. S. B. Leakey.)

The range of variation in the cranial capacity of the Australopithecinae is not certainly known, but it was evidently quite considerable. Two specimens from Sterkfontein (a skull and a natural endocranial cast) give fairly reliable estimates of 435 and 480
cc. A partial endocranial cast of another Sterkfontein skull (much
crushed) was estimated by Broom and Robinson to have had a
volume, when complete, of about 530 cc. The endocranial cast of
the immature Taung skull (the right half of which is almost complete) has an estimated volume of rather more than 500 cc. In
this individual the deciduous dentition was still in place, and the
first permanent molar had recently erupted. On the assumption
that the rate of brain growth in the Australopithecinae was equivalent to that of modern anthropoid apes, it may be estimated that
the cranial capacity of the adult Taung individual would have
approximated to 600 cc., with a theoretical upper limit (according to Zuckerman, 167) of 785 cc. The remains of the skull found
at Kromdraai do not permit of even an approximate estimation
of cranial capacity, but it is at least apparent from the size of the
endocranial casts of the preserved temporal and cerebellar regions
of the cranial wall that it must have exceeded that of the Sterkfontein specimens. The Swartkrans skulls and jaws are considerably larger than those found at Sterkfontein, but, unfortunately,
none of the calvariae are sufficiently well preserved to permit
accurate estimates of cranial capacity. So far as the available evidence now goes, it may be accepted on the basis of a careful
study by Tobias (143), that the range of variation in the Australopithecinae probably extended from about 450 cc. to over 600 cc.,
and "that even the most generous estimate yields a maximum
value of 848 cc. at the australopithecine grade of hominid organization." This compares with 752 cc. for the largest cranial capacity
of a gorilla so far recorded (125); but it needs to be recognized
that this was a large male animal, almost certainly exceeding the
body weight of most of the Australopithecinae.

In some of the discussions resulting from the first discoveries
of australopithecine skulls, rather unnecessary emphasis was
placed on the exact value of the cranial capacity, apparently on
the assumption that upon this character mainly depends the

question whether the Australopithecinae are to be regarded as representatives of the Pongidae or whether they are hominids of very primitive type. This assumption, again, seems to have been based upon the supposition that there is an arbitrary point in the expansion of the brain (some have suggested a cranial capacity of 750 or 800 cc.) which forms a sort of dividing line between man and ape. But (let us once more emphasize) the expansion of the brain to the size characteristic of the *later* Hominidae evidently did not occur until very long after this family had become segregated in the course of evolution from the Pongidae, and a large cranial capacity is thus not a diagnostic feature of the family Hominidae as a whole. In any case, of course, we know nothing of the intrinsic structure of the australopithecine brain, which, in spite of its relatively small size, may have had a more elaborate neural organization than that of the modern anthropoid apes.

Several natural endocranial casts of the Australopithecinae have so far been found, two almost complete specimens at Taung and Sterkfontein and two fragmentary specimens from Sterkfontein. Plaster casts have also been prepared of the endocranial cavity of skulls or portions of skulls found at Sterkfontein, Kromdraai, and Makapansgat. Most of these endocranial casts were studied in some detail by Schepers (20, 21); but, in his attempt to extract every possible item of information from them (perhaps excusable, considering the unique character at that time of these South African fossils), he undoubtedly allowed himself to overstep the limits of legitimate deduction and to read into the surface details of the casts morphological and physiological conclusions which are certainly not warranted by the facts. As might be expected from a consideration of the skulls, the general size and the main proportions of the australopithecine endocranial cast do not differ very markedly (at any rate, on superficial inspection) from those of large chimpanzees or gorillas; and their surface irregularities unfortunately do not provide very much information relating to those morphological details which are commonly regarded as of particular interest in contrasting the hominid with the ape cerebrum. But there are two points of relevance which may be mentioned here. In the first place, the "Sylvian notch" between the frontal lobe and the temporal pole is deeper and more sharply angulated than it is in the generality of modern large anthropoid apes of equivalent size, as is evident enough when direct comparisons are made between the actual endocranial casts (though it has been disputed by those who have relied only on diagrams and drawings). However, this is simply a reflection of the sharp, undercut character of the orbitosphenoid in the base of the skull, which, again, is evidently the result of the degree of flexure of the basis cranii shown by the australopithecine skull. By itself this character of the "Sylvian notch" does not necessarily, of course, provide any indication of enhanced cerebral development. The other feature is the richness and complexity of the convolutional impressions on the fossil endocranial casts. Although this character has been overemphasized by some writers, it is actually quite obtrusive. But comparisons with endocranial casts of modern anthropoid apes, *H. erectus,* and *H. sapiens* are not easy to make, for in all these types the convolutions do not imprint themselves on the endocranium nearly so distinctly. A direct visual comparison of the fossil casts with the actual brains of the large apes suggests that in the Australopithecinae the convolutional pattern of the cerebral hemispheres was probably more complex, but such a conclusion needs to be established by more detailed comparative studies before it can be accepted. Some emphasis has been laid on the posterior position and reduced size of the alleged "simian sulcus" in the occipital lobe of the brain, features which may in some sense be regarded as hominid, since they have been taken to indicate an expansion of the parietal cortex to a degree not found in the modern apes. It is really not possible to identify this sulcus with certainty from the impressions on the cast, but a careful examination of the original natural endocranial cast of the Taung skull does support the original contention of Dart that, in this particular individual at least, the simian sulcus must have been placed rather far back. For the sulcal impressions are sufficiently well marked to justify the negative conclusion that it did not occupy the relatively forward position in which it is commonly found in gorillas and chimpanzees. It will be apparent from what has been said that, taken by themselves, the endocranial

Australopithecus

casts of the Australopithecinae do not permit of firm statements regarding the convolutional pattern of the brain itself. But such indications as there are do appear to assume some significance when taken in conjunction with all the other anatomical characters of the skull, dentition, and limb skeleton.[6]

It has already been mentioned that the australopithecine skull is remarkably primitive in its *general* proportions, related to the combination of a small brain case with large jaws. This character, indeed, seems to have misled some of the earlier critics of Dart and Broom, for they failed to recognize that it is associated with a remarkable assemblage of morphological details in which, in combination, the skull contrasts strongly with that of the Pongidae and is to be matched only in the Hominidae. These hominid features may be listed as follows.

a) The Cranial Height.   One of the obtrusive features of the exceptionally well preserved australopithecine skull (No. V) from Sterkfontein is the height of the cranial vault above the level of the orbit (Figs. 13 and 15). This has been expressed by the "supra-orbital height index," which measures the height of the brain case above the level of the supra-orbital margin in relation to the total height above the Frankfurt plane (81). A comparison with a series of gorilla, chimpanzee, and orang skulls shows that in the Sterkfontein V skull the relative height exceeds the range of variation in anthropoid apes and actually comes within the range of hominid skulls.[7] It is not possible to assess with complete accuracy the supra-orbital height index in the other australopithecine skulls discovered in South Africa; but estimates based on reconstructions of the 1936 Sterkfontein skull (No. I) and of the two adult skulls from Swartkrans confirm the observation based on the Sterkfontein V skull. The high cranial vault in the australopithecine skull, it should be noted, is related, not to the actual size of the brain case, but to the fact that it is set higher in relation to

[6] For a critical discussion of the endocranial casts of the Australopithecinae discovered up to 1947 see Le Gros Clark (80).

[7] This statement was controverted on the basis of observations that in a few gorilla skulls the index approximates closely to that of the Sterkfontein skull. But these observations were based on measurements which most unfortunately included the sagittal crest in the cranial height of male gorillas (83).

the upper part of the facial skeleton. This, again, is evidently related to the flexure of the basicranial axis, which, being more marked than it is in the anthropoid apes, raises the brain case to a relatively higher level.

b) The Low Level of the Occipital Torus and Inion. This has been estimated on the basis of the "nuchal area height index" in the Sterkfontein skull V (Figs. 13 and 15). It shows that the occipital torus (in relation to the Frankfurt plane) occupies as low a level as it does in hominid skulls, and the index is far below the range of variation shown in the large anthropoid apes. As is well known, in adult apes the torus forms a crest reaching high up on the occipital aspect of the skull, thus extending very considerably the nuchal area for the attachment of the powerful neck muscles. On the other hand, in the Australopithecinae (as in *Homo*) the nuchal area is, by comparison, very restricted and, moreover, faces downward rather than backward on the occipital squama. That this was a consistent feature of the australopithecine skull is indicated by the appearance of the occipital region in other specimens. For example, the Olduvai skull and the well-preserved occipital bone of *Australopithecus* found at Makapansgat also show quite a small nuchal area, limited above by a comparatively weak torus. An examination of the crushed Sterkfontein skull I and the fragmentary Kromdraai skull provides similar evidence.

c) The Position of the Occipital Condyles. One of the features in which the hominid skull makes a strong contrast with the pongid skull is the forward position of the occipital condyles in relation (1) to the total skull length and (2) to the transverse level of the auditory apertures. In the Pongidae, in association with the different poise of the head during life, the condyles are situated a considerable way behind the mid-point of the cranial length and also well behind the auditory apertures, and it is interesting to note that the latter relationship holds good for the immature as well as the adult skull. In the Australopithecinae the relative position of the condyles has been accurately determined in the Sterkfontein skull V, and on the basis of the "condylar-position index" it can be shown that they are definitely farther forward in relation to the total cranial length than in adult orangs and chimpanzees[8] and the great majority of adult gorillas (Fig. 15). In the latter a few specimens have been found in which the "condylar-position index" equals or even exceeds that of the Sterkfontein skull. But in these instances the indices are not strictly comparable, for in large male gorillas the sagittal crest commonly extends backward beyond the brain case as an attenuated flange, which thus exaggerates the total skull length when the latter is expressed by the usual over-all measurement (83). In any case, it is important to recognize that the position of the condyles in relation to the skull length does not, of course, provide more than an approximate measure of the balance of the head in relation to the carriage of the body—to obtain such a measure accurately, we should require (*inter alia*) to know the position of the center of gravity of the whole head during life. It is also to be noted that, although the high condylar-position index indicates a relatively forward position of the condyles in the Sterkfontein skull, in relation to the total skull length they are not situated so far forward as in *Homo*. On the other hand, their forward position relative to the auditory apertures (and also to other elements of the skull base, such as the extremity of the petrous bone and the carotid foramen) parallels that of hominid skulls generally. This important relationship is consistently present in all the known australopithecine skulls in which the cranial base is sufficiently well preserved. Finally, apart from their relative position, it is to be observed that in the australopithecine skulls the long axis of the occipital condyles is approximately horizontal (in reference to the Frankfurt plane) as in hominid skulls, and does not slope upward and backward as it normally does in pongid skulls of equivalent size and massiveness.[9]

[8] In the pygmy chimpanzee, *P. paniscus*, the "condylar-position index" may approximate closely to that of the Sterkfontein V skull, but the skull of this species preserves an infantile form and is small and very lightly constructed; it is thus not directly comparable with the massive and heavily built australopithecine skull.

[9] It has been assumed that the condylar-position index *by itself* is always correlated with the degree of postural erectness. The fallacy of this assumption is exposed by the fact that the index varies quite considerably even in modern

The three hominid features of the australopithecine skull to which attention has just been drawn are evidently all related di-

---

H. sapiens. In extreme brachycephaly, for example, the occipital condyles may be placed considerably farther back in relation to the total skull length than in dolichocephalic skulls. But this can hardly be taken to mean that such brachycephalics do not habitually assume a fully erect posture!

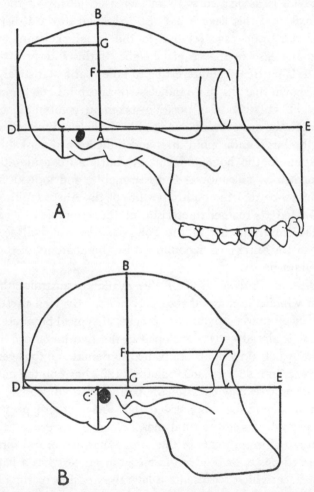

Fig. 15.—Outlines of skulls of *A*, a female gorilla, and *B*, *Australopithecus* (Sterkfontein skull V). The indices mentioned in the text are illustrated here: nuchal-area height index *AG/AB;* supra-orbital height index, *FB/AB;* condylar-position index, *CD/CE.* One-third natural size.

rectly or indirectly to a common factor—the poise of the head in relation to the vertebral column. The small nuchal area and the low position of the occipital torus provide clear evidence that the neck musculature was not extensively developed to hold up the head in relation to a forward-sloping cervical spine, as it is in the modern large anthropoid apes. The forward position of the occipital condyles is associated with an increased flexure of the basicranial axis, and this flexure has also led to an upward displacement of the brain case relative to the facial skeleton, with a resultant increase in the cranial height. If this interpretation is correct, it is particularly interesting to note that a statistical analysis has shown that the three indices—supra-orbital height, nuchal area height, and condylar position—taken in combination, definitely place the australopithecine skull outside the limits of variation of the large anthropoid apes and indicate a remarkable approximation to the hominid skull. And if due consideration is given to their significance, it is a reasonable, and indeed an obvious, inference that the bodily posture of the Australopithecinae approximated to that characteristic of the Hominidae and was very different from that of the Pongidae. As we shall see, the validity of this inference is confirmed by the anatomy of the pelvis and limb bones.

d) *Mastoid Process.* In all the available australopithecine skulls in which the mastoid region is sufficiently well preserved, there is a well-marked pyramidal process of typical hominid form. Indeed, it is already well developed in the two immature Swartkrans skulls (of individuals equivalent in dental age to seven and eleven years in modern man). Schultz (122) has pointed out that a mastoid process may occasionally be found in adult male gorillas, but it should be emphasized that, even where present, it differs markedly from the total morphological pattern which the hominid structure presents in the latter's sharply conical form, its well-defined posterior border (in apes the process has a flat posterior surface which represents a lateral extension of the nuchal area of the occiput), its flat medial surface bounded by a digastric fossa, and the details of its immediate relationship to the posterior margin of the auditory aperture. It also needs to be emphasized that, unlike that of the gorilla, the mastoid process appears to be a consistent (and not an occasional, sporadic) element of the australopithecine skull, and also that it is present even in the young, immature skull.

It is not possible to be certain of the functional significance of the hominid type of mastoid process in the australopithecine skull. Probably it is related to the relative degree of development and the direction of pull of the several muscles attached to it, and this is presumably associated with the balance of the head on the spinal column. But it may also simply be a concomitant of the complex morphological changes which have affected the base of the skull and the relationships of its component elements.

e) *The Frontal and Upper Facial Regions.* The contour of the forehead and supra-orbital eminences, combined with the orientation of the orbital apertures, the high level of the zygomatic arch, and the abbreviated temporal process of the zygomatic bone, comprise (in Sterkfontein skull V) a total morphological pattern which is quite surprisingly hominid and which does not appear to be paralleled in any pongid skull of equivalent size. It is even evident in the immature Taung skull. In the Sterkfontein skull I, the pattern appears also to have been closely similar (so far as can be determined from a reconstruction of this crushed specimen); but in the large Swartkrans and Olduvai skulls the frontal region is considerably flattened, as it also is in some of the skulls of *Homo erectus*.

f) *The Mandibular Fossa.* It has often been assumed that the type of movement which occurs at the mandibular joint can be determined by a study of the construction of the mandibular fossa of the skull. To a limited extent this is true, but the problem is complicated by the fact that in life the fossa and the condyle of the mandible are separated by an interposed fibrous disk of variable shape and thickness, which also needs to be taken into consideration because of the part it plays in the mechanics of the joint movements. No doubt the best indication of the nature of the jaw movements in the Australopithecinae is provided by the teeth and their mode of attrition. As we shall see, the dentition does give evidence of jaw movements similar to those of *Homo,* and it

141

is particularly interesting, therefore, that the mandibular fossa also shows a combination of features of a hominid rather than a pongid type.

The mandibular fossa is especially well preserved in the Kromdraai skull, and in the details of its construction it conforms entirely with the hominid type. These details include a relatively deep articular concavity, bounded anteriorly by a prominent, transversely disposed, articular eminence; a postglenoid process of small size, which thus exposes the tympanic bone so that the latter forms practically the whole extent of the posterior wall of the fossa as a flattened, slightly concave, rectangular plate with a relatively sharp lower border; and no more than a slight indication of an entoglenoid process. In the Sterkfontein skulls V and VIII much the same construction is also found, except that the postglenoid process is more strongly developed (but a flattened tympanic plate still enters into the formation of the posterior wall of the mandibular fossa), and the same applies to the large Swartkrans skulls. Finally, the hollow of the mandibular fossa in all these specimens extends up to a consistently high level in relation to the auditory aperture, in some specimens reaching as high as the upper border of the latter (in the Pondigae the articular surface is almost invariably placed at a much lower level). All these constructional items of the mandibular fossa in the Australopithecinae (and particularly in the Kromdraai specimen) comprise a total morphological pattern of a hominid type which has not been shown to occur in any of the known anthropoid apes. It is clearly a pattern of some intricacy, involving several different osseous elements, and may thus be regarded as of some importance for the morphological evidence it provides in assessing the affinities of the australopithecines.

SUTURES

Certain authorities have laid considerable emphasis on variations of sutural pattern which they believe to differentiate the Hominidae from the Pongidae, in particular, the arrangement of the sutures in the pterionic region of the temporal fossa, the medial wall of the orbit, and the anterior fossa of the cranial cavity. In fact, however, these sutural patterns show some variation in each of the two families, and, so far as individual specimens are concerned, they cannot, therefore, be regarded as diagnostic. But it is of interest to note that in the australopithecine skull these patterns appear to conform to the normal hominid condition, i.e., there is a sphenoparietal contact in the temporal fossa (reported to occur in at least three specimens), while an ethmolachrymal contact in the orbit and a sphenoethmoidal contact in the anterior fossa were probably present (according to Broom) in the Sterkfontein skull V (20). None of these sutural patterns is normally found in the African anthropoid apes (though they may all occur as occasional exceptions); on the other hand, they are normally present in the orang. Thus although, taken in combination, they suggest a significant contrast with the African apes, they do not, of course, serve to differentiate the Australopithecinae from the Pongidae as a whole.

The high level of the temporoparietal suture on the cranial wall in the Australopithecinae is an indication of an expanded temporal squama, wherein these fossils show a rather obtrusive hominid character, for the relative size of this element is much smaller in the Pongidae than in the Hominidae. In anthropoid ape skulls examined by the present writer the summit of the temporal squama was not found to extend above the horizontal level of the supraorbital margin in the Frankfurt plane. But this is a well-marked feature of the Sterkfontein skull V, in which the temporoparietal suture is very clearly seen.

Another suture which has been held to be of peculiar significance in connection with the relationships of the Hominidae is that related to the facial component of the premaxilla. This component is always found in the Pongidae (as in mammals generally) and in young individuals forms that part of the upper jaw in which the incisor teeth are implanted. In *H. sapiens* the premaxilla, as a separate element, does not normally enter into the formation of the facial surface of the upper jaw, for early in embryonic development it becomes fused with the maxilla. Indeed, it has been accepted for many years that during embryonic development the human premaxilla disappears altogether from the facial surface of the skull by submergence following an overgrowth of the maxillary elements, and this was regarded by some authorities as a peculiarly hominid distinction of great taxonomic significance. However, the embryological studies of Noback and Moss (100) seem to make it clear that the premaxillary and maxillary bones actually fuse ectofacially in the human embryo, as, in fact, they do in early postnatal life in the anthropoid apes. It has been argued that this embryonic fusion of the premaxilla is a fundamental distinction of the Hominidae, the implied assumption being that its early occurrence in the human embryo indicates a correspondingly ancient phylogenetic history. But such an argument is based on a *non sequitur,* for even a geologically recent mutation may find expression in the earliest phases of ontogeny. It is not improbable, indeed, that the reduction of the facial premaxilla may have been related to the recession of the jaws during quite a late stage in the hominid sequence of evolution, possibly even in the Early Pleistocene. The fact that the facial component of the premaxilla (with an extensive premaxillary suture extending up to the narial margin) has occasionally been observed in the skull of the newborn Negro clearly indicates that its genetic basis has by no means disappeared, even in *H. sapiens.*

THE ENDOCRANIAL ASPECT OF THE SKULL BASE

In the well-preserved Sterkfontein skull V, Broom was able to clear away the stalagmitic incrustations within the cranial cavity and make an almost complete exposure of the skull base. The hominid features to which he drew attention here include the sharply undercut anterior margin of the middle cranial fossa (evidently related to a degree of flexure of the basis cranii not found in the large anthropoid apes), the comparatively shallow depression containing the cribriform plate of the ethmoid, the prominent (and bifid) anterior clinoid process, and the deep pituitary fossa.

JAWS AND PALATE

The upper jaw and palate of the Australopithecinae show the marked reduction and recession of the incisor region characteristic of the hominid skull, with an evenly rounded alveolar margin.

The recession of the incisor region is also evident in the numerous specimens of the mandible which have been collected. The symphysial surface of the mandible is almost flat and vertical in the upper part of its extent, and in some specimens there is even a slight mental eminence. There is no "simian shelf," and sagittal sections of the symphysial region show a remarkable resemblance to that of the large *H. erectus* mandible (*"Meganthropus"*). The "simian shelf," it may be noted, is also absent in the Early Miocene representatives of the Pongidae; it was evidently a later development in the evolutionary sequence of this family. The mental foramen is frequently single (in contrast to the multiple foramina characteristic of anthropoid apes), particularly in the Swartkrans specimens, and does not occupy the low position characteristic of the pongid mandible. As in the upper jaw, the contour of the alveolar border is definitely hominid in type and quite different from that of any known group of apes, living or extinct.

Apart from the hominid features of the australopithecine skull listed above, a close study of some of the original specimens shows a number of other details which, though *individually* variable in both hominids and pongids, present, all together, a combination which still further emphasizes the hominid affinities of these South African fossils. Such details include the contour and construction of the supra-orbital ridge, the relatively short and wide basiocciput, the angulation between the tympanic and petrous bones, the presence (usually) of a single infra-orbital foramen, the inclination of the foramen magnum, the well-developed lingular process in the young mandible (a small process of bone overlapping the foramen on the inner aspect of the vertical ramus of the mandible), the disposition of some of the foramina in the cranial base, and so forth. Taken individually, as isolated abstractions, some of these features may not have a significant taxonomic relevance. But if they are all taken in combination with one another and with those features which are not to be found in any known group of pongids, they have a very high degree of taxonomic relevance, for they quite clearly comprise a total morphological pattern of the hominid, and not the pongid, type. On the basis of the skull structure alone, therefore, the proposition

145

that the Australopithecinae actually represent an early phase in
the hominid sequence of evolution appears to be well founded.
Indeed, it may well be asked why this rather obvious interpretation of the skull structure was so vigorously contested when it
was first put forward. One reason, as we have already pointed
out, is that the earlier critics of Dart and Broom seem to have
assumed that the absolute size of the brain by itself provides the
final taxonomic criterion of distinction between the Pongidae and
the Hominidae, which, of course, is by no means the case (see
p. 11). Other features of the australopithecine skull which are
mainly the secondary concomitants of a small brain case associated with large jaws, such as the marked prognathism and the
development in some of the larger skulls of a small sagittal crest,
were also taken to indicate pongid affinities, in spite of the fact
that they must also be presumed to have been present in the earlier phases of the hominid sequence of evolution (i.e., before the
rapid expansion of the brain to the size characteristic of *Homo*
had begun to manifest itself). Mention has already been made
of the sagittal crest in the Swartkrans skulls (see p. 44), and it is
necessary only to reiterate here that such a crest is not to be regarded as a morphological entity in itself with a separate genetic
basis—it is the result of the upward growth on the side of the
skull of temporal muscles which, in large adults, require an area
of attachment more extensive than can be provided by the brain
case itself. In any case, the crest (in those individuals in which it
is developed) is very different from the sagittal crest which may
be found in male gorillas, orangs, and (very occasionally) chimpanzees, in that it did not extend back into a high nuchal crest.
This is a point which needs to be emphasized, for it had been
argued (on the basis of one skull in which the occipital region is
missing) that, since the crest must have been similar to that of a
gorilla, the missing occiput must have shown a high nuchal crest;
therefore the area for the nuchal musculature was very extensive;
and therefore the head was held forward in a position incompatible with an erect posture. But the initial assumption which
formed the starting point for this sequence of speculations has
proved to be incorrect. For, without exception, in all the several
occipital bones of the Australopithecinae which have now been

discovered, the nuchal ridge is low and the nuchal area of limited extent, precisely as in hominid skulls (see Figs. 15 and 16) and very different from gorilla skulls. This is the case with the Olduvai skull, and according to a report by Dr. Robinson, it applies equally well to two skulls from Swartkrans with a small sagittal crest; in these specimens the occipital region is sufficiently well preserved to make it quite certain that here, also, no nuchal crest of the gorilloid type was present. Indeed, one of the specimens shows that the sagittal crest does not even extend back as far as the occipital bone. It needs to be recognized, of course, that the shelflike nuchal crest of the gorilla is not produced by the temporal muscle alone, but by the opposed growth of the temporal and nuchal muscles *together*. If, with the assumption of an erect posture, the nuchal musculature is reduced (as it is in the Hominidae) a shelflike nuchal crest is hardly to be expected.

DENTITION

The dentition of the Australopithecinae has been studied in more detail than any other remains of these extinct creatures. There are several reasons for this. (1) Teeth have been found in great number and in many cases excellently preserved. Apart from the permanent teeth, several examples of tho deciduous dentition are also known. (2) The morphological characters of the dentition have proved to be of the greatest value for taxonomic determinations in the study of mammalian paleontology generally, and there is every reason to suppose that this applies as well to the Hominoidea as to other groups of mammals. (3) Because statements regarding the hominid features of the dentition were strongly contested by some critics, it became necessary to restudy all the teeth in greater detail, in order to solve the conflict of opinion. It would be superfluous here to give a comprehensive account of the dental morphology of the Australopithecinae, for this information is available in readily accessible publications (19, 20, 21, 82, 113, 114, 118). That it conforms essentially to the hominid type may best be demonstrated by first listing and contrasting the fundamental characters which distinguish the Hominidae (as represented by *Homo*) from the Pongidae (Table 1).

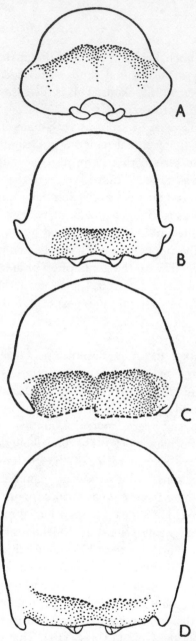

Fig. 16.—Occipital view of the skull of *A*, a chimpanzee; *B, Australopithecus* (Sterkfontein skull V); *C, Homo erectus* (*Pithecanthropus*) (after Weiden-reich); *D, Homo sapiens* (European). One-third natural size. All the skulls have been oriented on the Frankfurt plane. Note the high level of the nuchal crest in the chimpanzee skull—a typical pongid character.

148

TABLE 1

PONGIDAE	HOMINIDAE

PERMANENT DENTITION

Pongidae	Hominidae
The canine and postcanine teeth form approximately straight rows, parallel or slightly divergent anteriorly, and (with very rare exceptions) the upper dental arcade is interrupted by a diastemic interval related to the canines.	The dental arcade has an evenly curved contour of parabolic or elliptical form, with no diastemic interval (except to a slight degree in some individuals of *H. erectus*).
The incisors are hypertrophied and relatively broad (at least in the Recent genera of the large anthropoid apes). The sockets of the upper central incisors are placed well in front of the level of the anterior margin of the canine sockets (with occasional exceptions where the canines form unusually large tusks, e.g., in some large male gorillas).	The incisors avoid gross hypertrophy and thus retain more primitive proportions. The posterior margins of the sockets of the upper central incisors are on a level with, or behind, the anterior margins of the canine sockets.
The canines are relatively large, conical, and sharply pointed, with a well-marked internal cingulum commonly prolonged back (in the lower canine) into a talonid. The upper and lower canines overlap to a marked degree in occlusion; at an early stage of attrition they show facets on the anterior and posterior aspects of the crown and remain projecting well beyond the occlusal level of the postcanine teeth (except only in very aged individuals, where all the teeth show an advanced state of extreme attrition or where the canine crowns may have been accidentally broken off during life). The canines show a pronounced sexual dimorphism.	The canines are relatively small, spatulate, and bluntly pointed, with the internal cingulum reduced to an inconspicuous basal tubercle. They wear down flat from the tip only and at an early stage of attrition do not project beyond the occlusal level of the postcanine teeth (except in some individuals of *H. erectus*). The canines show no pronounced sexual dimorphism.

149

The first upper premolar normally has three roots.

The first upper premolar commonly has one or two roots only, but in some modern races of *H. sapiens* a small percentage show three roots.

The anterior lower premolar is sectorial in character, commonly set obliquely to the axis of the tooth row, and with two roots. It is predominantly unicuspid, but it may have a rudimentary lingual cusp set on the lower slope of the large buccal cusp. In early stages of wear it shows an attrition facet on the anterolateral surface of the crown. There are no well-defined anterior and posterior foveae.

The anterior lower premolar is of a bicuspid type, with the cusps set in an approximately transverse plane. The two cusps are subequal in primitive hominids, such as *H. erectus;* but in *H. sapiens* the lingual cusp has undergone a secondary reduction. In primitive hominids the anterior and posterior foveae are sharply defined.

The molar teeth show considerable variation in their cusp pattern and in their absolute and relative dimensions. Except in advanced attrition (or rarely in abnormal specimens in which the canines have been accidentally broken off), the occlusal aspect does not become worn down to an even flat surface. In primitive pongids of Miocene and Pliocene age the first lower molar is relatively small.

The molar teeth show considerable variation in their cusp pattern and in their absolute and relative dimensions. In general, the cusps tend to be more rounded and more closely compacted than in the Pongidae. In *H. erectus* the second upper molar is larger than the first, and the last lower molar often greater in length than the second. In *H. sapiens* the second and third molars have undergone a secondary reduction. Even in early stages of attrition, the occlusal aspects of the molars commonly become worn down to an even flat surface.

The canines erupt late, after the second molar and sometimes even after the third molar.

The canines erupt early, normally before the second molar (though a later eruption is stated to occur in *H. erectus, H. neanderthalensis,* and in certain modern races of *H. sapiens*).

DECIDUOUS DENTITION

The lower canines are conical and sharply pointed, projecting well beyond the level of the milk molars, with an approximately straight internal cingulum extending back to form a talonid. The first lower molars are sectorial in type, with the crown mainly composed of a single, large, pointed cusp (the protoconid) and a depressed talonid. There is no well-marked anterior fovea. The dental arcade is U-shaped.

The lower canines are spatulate in form, not projecting markedly beyond the level of the milk molars, relatively short and bluntly pointed, and with no projecting talonid. The first lower molars are multi-cuspid, with four or five cusps disposed at approximately the same level. There is usually a well-marked anterior fovea.

The dental arcade forms an even parabolic or elliptical curve.

The differential characters of the dentition listed in Table 1 are those which, on the basis of the comparative study of large numbers of hominids and pongids (both Recent and fossil), have been established to have a high degree of taxonomic relevance. Taken together, they comprise total morphological patterns of considerable complexity, which are distinctive of each of the two families. For the problem of the assessment of the affinities of the Australopithecinae, therefore, it is of particular importance to note that the total morphological pattern of the dentition of these fossil hominoids conforms to that of the Hominidae (Fig. 17). In all the adult specimens so far discovered, the dental arcade is evenly curved, with no diastemic intervals; the upper incisors are consistently small and retracted to the level of the canines; the latter are reduced in size and spatulate in form, show no very obtrusive sexual dimorphism, and, in the earliest stages of attrition, without exception became worn down flat from the tip to the level of the adjacent teeth; the anterior upper premolars have two roots (of which one may in some individuals be partially subdivided); the anterior lower premolars are of the nonsectorial bicuspid type (with the lingual almost as large as the buccal cusp) and have one root marked on the surface by longitudinal grooves which suggest a fusion of two roots; the molar teeth in the detailed morphology of their cusps show a much closer re-

151

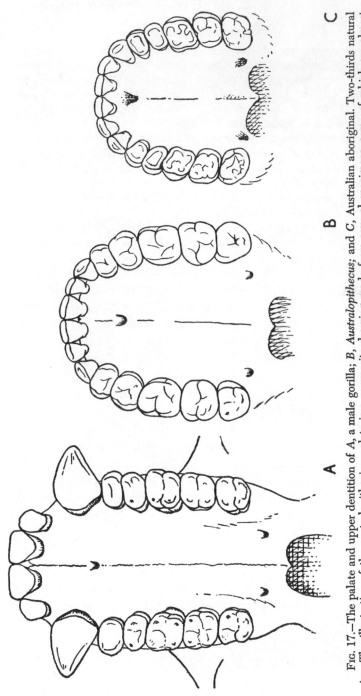

Fig. 17.—The palate and upper dentition of A, a male gorilla; B, *Australopithecus*; and C, Australian aboriginal. Two-thirds natural size. The illustration of the australopithecine palate is a composite drawing made from several specimens, some of which are almost complete. (For illustrations of eight specimens of the australopithecine palate and upper dentition see Le Gros Clark, 82.) Note in *Australopithecus* the relatively small canine and incisors, the absence of a diastema, and the evenly curved dental arcade. (By courtesy of the Trustees of the British Museum.)

semblance to the primitive hominid *H. erectus* than to any known type of pongid;[10] and in the earliest stages of attrition they became worn down to an even flat surface. It is particularly important to recognize that these statements are not based on isolated and individual teeth but on a considerable number of specimens (in some cases with the whole upper or lower dentition complete or almost complete). The same applies to the deciduous dentition, of which there are at least four specimens (apart from isolated teeth). The milk canine is quite distinct from that of anthropoid apes, and the first milk molar is a complex tooth with four or five cusps at approximately the same level on the crown and a well-marked anterior fovea. The differentiation of australopithecine from ape canine teeth (both permanent and deciduous), which is so obviously apparent on direct visual comparison, has been fully demonstrated by the statistical analysis of appropriate measurements (82). The results of the multivariate analysis by Bronowski and Long (13, 14, 15) are particularly revealing, for example, in their demonstration that, for all the milk canines so far discovered at that time, the discriminant functions which they calculated fall well outside the range of modern anthropoid apes and actually lie within the range of *Homo*.

Finally, there is good evidence from the study of the dentition in immature specimens that the order of eruption of the permanent teeth conforms to that of the Hominidae. It may be noted that in the ascending scale of Primates there is a progressive acceleration in the replacement of the deciduous dentition relative to the eruption of the permanent molars, associated with a prolongation of the growth period. In the Pongidae the canine teeth are still very late in their replacement, often not completing

10 It is a significant commentary on the close relationship of the Pongidae and the Hominidae that in some groups the molar teeth may be exceedingly difficult to distinguish with absolute certainty. The prolonged controversy on the molar teeth of the famous Piltdown jaw (quite apart from the faked fabrication of the hominid type of wear) is sufficient to make this clear. But, as far as the australopithecine molars are concerned, while in the details of their cusp morphology they can readily be distinguished from all the known genera of apes, it would be extremely difficult to distinguish them from molars of the *H. erectus* group of hominids.

their eruption until after that of the last molar and, in any case, not until the second molar has completed its eruption. The late eruption of the canine was retained in certain fossil hominids (e.g., *H. erectus*) and is still retained even in some groups of *H. sapiens*. But in most modern races the canine erupts before the second molar, and the first incisor tooth may occasionally erupt even before the first permanent molar. According to Schultz (120), this occasional early eruption of the first incisor is a unique feature in which the Hominidae contrast with all other Primates. From the material collected at Swartkrans, it is evident that in this group of Australopithecinae the order of dental eruption actually corresponds to that normally found in *H. sapiens* (i.e., the canines erupted before the second molar), and in one specimen the first incisor has even erupted before the first permanent molar. On the other hand, the immature mandible found at Makapansgat shows that in this particular specimen the canine erupted after the second molar (as in *H. erectus* and some modern human races). The important point to emphasize, however, is that the pattern of dental replacement characteristic of *H. sapiens*, and also present in some of the Australopithecinae, has not been found to occur in any of the Pongidae, Recent or extinct.

Although the australopithecine dentition is thus essentially of the hominid type, it differs from that of *H. sapiens* in a number of significant features. For example, the premolar and molar teeth are of large size, the third lower molar (though showing considerable variation in its proportions) commonly exceeds in length that of the second molar, and in the anterior lower premolar the lingual cusp is relatively large. But these are evidently primitive hominid characters, for they are also found in *H. erectus*. The absolute and relative size of the premolars and molars in the Australopithecinae is rather variable. For example, they are more massive in the Kromdraai and Swartkrans specimens than some of those recovered from Sterkfontein. Indeed, in an upper jaw from the latter site found in 1936, the teeth correspond in their dimensions almost precisely (i.e., to within 0.5 mm.) to those of the *H. erectus* maxilla found in Java in 1939 (81). On the other hand, the large lower premolars and molars of the

Morphological Characters

Swartkrans material show a most remarkable similarity in size, proportions, and cusp pattern to the equivalent teeth of the large 1941 mandible of *H. erectus* (= *"Meganthropus"*), as shown by the detailed comparative studies of Robinson (114). There is thus no reason to question the hominid status in the Australopithecinae on the basis of the over-all dimensions of the teeth of the premolar-molar series. Even if the large 1941 mandible is excluded, the diagram in Figure 18 makes it clear that the dif-

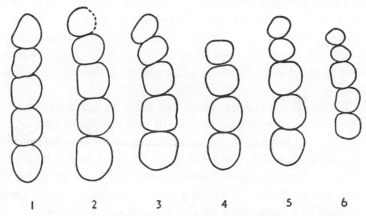

Fig. 18.—Outlines (partly after von Koenigswald) of the lower molars and premolars of *1*, an orang; *2* and *3*, australopithecine specimens from Kromdraai and Sterkfontein; *4, H. erectus* (mandible B); *5*, Australian aboriginal; and *6*, European. Two-thirds natural size. Compare the difference between the over-all dimensions of the australopithecine teeth and those of *H. erectus* with the differences which occur within the limits of the single species *Homo sapiens*.

ference in absolute size between these teeth in *H. erectus* and the Australopithecinae is actually less than the range of variation to be found in the single species *H. sapiens*. The fact is that, while the over-all dimensions of the molar and premolar teeth may have considerable taxonomic relevance in distinguishing species or even genera, they have in this case little or no taxonomic relevance for interfamilial distinctions.[11] Reference may be made here to

[11] It seems desirable to re-emphasize this rather obvious point, for in a statistical paper by Ashton and Zuckerman (3) it was claimed, on the basis of the over-all dimensions of length and breadth of the premolars and molars, that the australopithecine teeth "in their metrical attributes . . . are more ape-like than human," the implication being that in this respect they are pongid rather

two fragments of mandibles found at Swartkrans with molar teeth considerably smaller than the other specimens found at this site. On the basis of the first fragment (found in 1949) which contained the three molar teeth, a new genus, *Telanthropus,* was created by Broom and Robinson (17). However, the teeth are large by modern human standards, and they show resemblances to the other known australopithecine teeth (particularly in the relative size of the last molar). It may be, therefore, that *"Telanthropus"* represents merely the extreme limits of variation in the size of the teeth in the Australopithecinae (see p. 170). In the second *"Telanthropus"* jaw fragment, only the first and second molars are preserved, and they are unfortunately too severely worn to provide satisfactory information on their morphological details.

The dental characters which we have so far considered are familial characters which appear to indicate quite conclusively that, so far as reliance is placed on the criteria of dental morphology, the Australopithecinae are to be allocated to the Hominidae and not to the Pongidae. But the australopithecine dentition also shows certain generic characters which distinguish it from more advanced representatives of the Hominidae. These include the degree of reduction in size of the incisors and canines, so that they are disproportionately small in comparison with the premolar-molar series; the small size of the anterior relatively to the posterior premolar tooth (at least in the Swartkrans specimens); the variability and complexity of the enamel folds in the molar teeth; and the cusp pattern of the first milk molar. It is a characteristic of the Hominidae (in contrast to the Pongidae) that the

---

than hominid. The statistical methods used by these authors have been criticized on general grounds elsewhere (13 and 82); but one of the main criticisms of this paper is that for their comparisons with the Hominidae they referred only to measurements of the teeth of *H. sapiens.* Apart from this, however, it is of some considerable importance to note (in making reference to the paper) that, as Yates and Healy (164) later showed, the standard deviations recorded in it have been incorrectly calculated and the conclusions based on them are therefore invalid. In a later communication Ashton and Zuckerman (4) corrected this error and, as a result, were able to state that some of the dimensions which they had previously reported as not significantly different from those of Recent apes are, in fact, very different indeed.

first milk molar has undergone a marked degree of "molarization" —that is to say, it has developed four or five cusps, which make it resemble the typical multicuspid molar tooth. In the Australopithecinae this process of "molarization" seems actually to have proceeded farther than in *H. erectus* and *H. sapiens*. It has been argued that this is a specialization, possibly of a specific nature, suggesting that the Australopithecinae (or at least the South African representatives of this group) represent a collateral branch of the Hominidae which could hardly be ancestral to *Homo*.

THE LIMB SKELETON

As we have already noted (p. 14), there is reason to suppose that the primary factor which determined the evolutionary segregation of the Hominidae from the Pongidae (probably in the Miocene or Early Pliocene) was the divergent modification of the limbs in adaptation to erect bipedalism. The evidence of *H. erectus*, for example, provides a rather positive indication that the lower limbs had become perfected for a fully erect posture and gait while the morphological features of the skull still retained a number of primitive characters approximating in some respects to a simian level of development. If, then, the Australopithecinae are representatives of the hominid rather than the pongid sequence of evolution, the limb skeleton might be expected to be particularly relevant for the determination of their taxonomic status. In fact, this is the case. For example, several specimens of the australopithecine pelvic skeleton have been found in South Africa, and they are consistent in their fundamentally hominid construction, as they are also in certain details in which they differ from the pelvis of modern *H. sapiens*.

The first pelvic bone was found in 1947 in the stalagmitic breccia of the Sterkfontein site, in direct association with fragments of a femur and tibia, some vertebrae, and a crushed australopithecine skull, and within a few feet of other skulls, cranial fragments and numerous teeth of the same creatures. Later, almost the whole of this pelvis was assembled, including the os innominatum of each side, the sacrum, and also (in an articulated condition) some of the associated thoracic and lumbar vertebrae

(Fig. 21). Another specimen was found in 1948 at Makapansgat from a zone of breccia which had previously yielded an adolescent mandible of *Australopithecus*. Since this pelvic bone was also that of an adolescent, it may be presumed almost certainly to have belonged to the same individual as the mandible. A considerable part of an australopithecine pelvis was also discovered in 1950 at Swartkrans close to the remains of three skulls and associated with the lower half of a humerus. The Sterkfontein and Swartkrans specimens have been figured and briefly described by Broom and Robinson (19, 20). The Makapansgat pelvis, which consists of the ilium and the detached ischial portion, was described in detail by Dart. More recently a second australopithecine ilium has been found in breccia from the same site (37).

The hominid construction of the australopithecine pelvis shown by these specimens (Figs. 19, 20, and 21) is marked by the relative breadth of the ilium; the backward extension of the posterior extremity of the iliac crest and the low position of the sacral articulation in relation to the acetabulum; the orientation of the sacral articulation relatively to the vertical axis of the os innominatum; the sharply angulated sciatic notch associated with a prominent ischial spine; the strongly developed anterior inferior iliac spine; the orientation and position of the ischial tuberosity in relation to the acetabulum (particularly in the first Makapansgat specimen); and the well-marked groove on the ventral surface of the ilium for the ilio-psoas muscle. In all these characters, even individually, the pelvic bone makes a strong contrast with the modern anthropoid apes, and, taken in combination, they comprise a total morphological pattern which is distinctive of the Hominidae among all other groups of mammals. Moreover, they are characters which are quite certainly related to posture. The broad ilium extends the anteroposterior attachment of the gluteal musculature (of the buttock) which is used for balancing the trunk on the lower limbs; the bending-down of the posterior extremity of the iliac crest brings the gluteus maximus muscle to a position behind (instead of lateral to) the hip joint and so permits it to play its essential role as an extensor in walking erect (see Washburn, 148); the approximation of the sacral articular

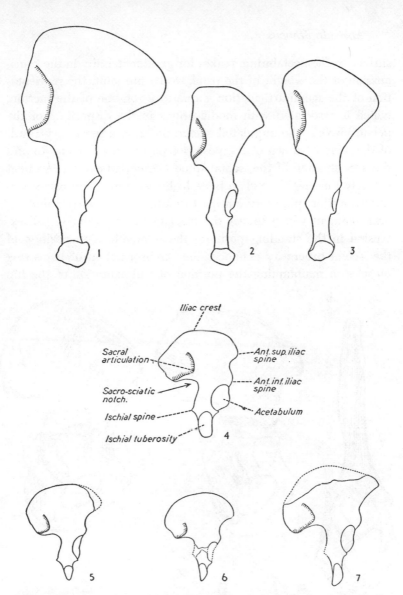

FIG. 19.—Lateral view of three specimens of the australopithecine pelvic bone (5, from Sterkfontein; 6, from Makapansgat; 7, from Swartkrans) compared with those of *Homo sapiens* (4) and the modern large apes (1, gorilla; 2, chimpanzee; 3, orang). One-sixth natural size. The position of the ventral margin of the area of contact with the sacrum on the inner aspect of the bone has been indicated. Note that in its fundamental characters the australopithecine bone conforms to the hominid pattern. On the other hand, it contrasts strongly with the apes (this has been confirmed by comparison with 87 pelvic bones of the modern large apes).

surface to the acetabulum makes for greater stability in the transmission of the weight of the trunk to the hip joint; the reorientation of the sacral articulation is due to a rotation of the sacrum, which is associated with modifications in the disposition of the pelvic viscera; the angulated sciatic notch is a secondary result of the bending-down of the posterior part of the dorsum ilii and the accentuation of the ischial spine (which attaches a ligament strongly binding the pelvic bone to the sacrum); the robust anterior inferior spine serves in part to attach the powerful iliofemoral ligament which braces the front of the hip joint in full extension in the standing position; the relatively high position of the ischial tuberosity enhances the extensor action of hamstring muscles in maintaining the position of full extension of the hip

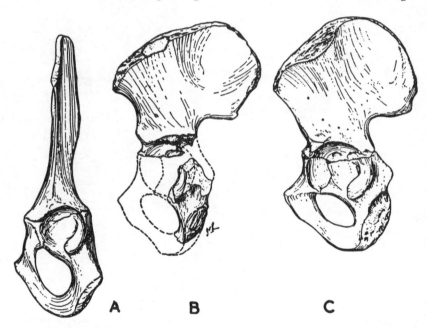

FIG. 20.—Left lateral views of the innominate bones of *A*, an adolescent chimpanzee; *B*, an adolescent specimen of *Australopithecus* found at Makapansgat; and *C*, an adolescent bushman. Note the outstanding hominid characters of the fossil specimen displayed by the relative breadth and orientation of the ilium, the sharply angulated sciatic notch, the strong development of the anterior inferior iliac spine, and the proximity of the ischial tuberosity to the acetabular socket. (From R. A. Dart, Am. J. Phys. Anthropol., Vol. **7**, 1949.)

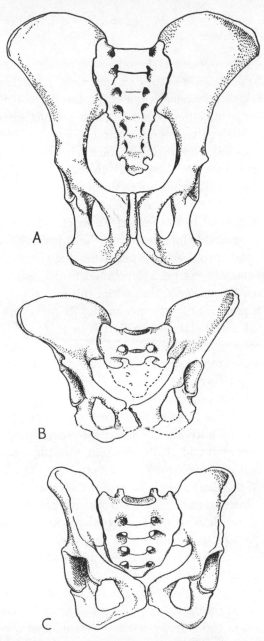

Fig. 21.—The pelvis of *A*, a chimpanzee; *B*, *Australopithecus;* and *C*, a bushman. All are drawn to the same scale from a photograph kindly supplied by Dr. J. T. Robinson. It is to be noted that, except for the lower half of the sacrum, the australopithecine pelvis (found at Sterkfontein in South Africa) is virtually complete, for those parts which were missing on one side of the fossil specimen have fortunately been preserved on the other side. (From *The Antecedents of Man* [Edinburgh University Press].)

by bringing their upper attachments to a position behind, rather than below, the hip joint in the erect position (in anthropoid apes, and in pronograde mammals generally, the greater distance between the tuberosity and the hip joint permits greater power when the hamstrings are brought into use with the hindlimb acting as a propulsive lever rather than a propulsive strut, 50); the deep groove for the ilio-psoas muscle is related to the fact that in the habitually extended position of the thigh in the erect posture the muscle has to turn backward at a marked angle to reach its attachment to the femur. From considerations such as these it is a reasonable inference that the Australopithecinae had become adapted to an erect bipedalism, though there are indications that this had not been developed to the perfection shown in *H. sapiens*. For example, the ischial tuberosity (at least in the Sterkfontein and Swartkrans specimens) is not quite so closely approximated to the acetabulum as it is in *H. sapiens,* the region of the anterior superior spine extends farther forward, and the area for the attachment of the strong sacroiliac ligaments is relatively not so extensive.

The functional implications of the australopithecine pelvic bone receive further corroboration from other parts of the lower-limb skeleton which have been found. Two specimens of the lower end of the femur found at Sterkfontein (16, 21) show a similar combination of morphological characters, e.g., the obliquity and robustness of the shaft, the alignment of the condyles, the contour of the patellar surfaces, and the forward prolongation of the intercondylar notch, which, taken together, comprise a total morphological pattern that conforms to the hominid femur and presumably also represents a mechanical adaptation related to erect bipedalism. The disposition of the intercondylar notch by itself must be regarded as highly significant, for it is difficult of explanation except on the assumption that (as in *Homo*) it served to accommodate the anterior cruciate ligament of the knee joint in the habitually extended position associated with an erect posture (80). A statistical analysis of the fragmentary first Sterkfontein femoral extremity soon after its discovery had already shown that it was very different from that of an anthropoid ape (63); but at that time some doubt was expressed whether its morphological features provided final evidence of an erect, rather than a quadrupedal, posture. However, the study of this very limited material was carried out before the reports of the specimens of the pelvic skeleton were available to show quite clearly that the Australopithecinae were certainly not quadrupedal creatures. The discovery of some upper extremities of the femur has also been reported, but from the brief accounts which have been published they appear to yield only limited information. In one specimen there are certain "gorilloid" features such as the relatively small size of the articular head. A tibia and fibula found in association with the australopithecine skull ("*Zinjanthropus*") at Olduvai have relatively straight shafts, and a report by Davis (38) leads to the conclusion that bony adaptation to bipedalism was well advanced at the ankle joint. However, from the evidence available it appears that the knee joint was less well adapted to bipedalism than it is in *H. sapiens*. A fragmentary ankle bone (talus) from Kromdraai shows an interesting combination of hominid and pongid features, and the former have been interpreted as modifications permitting a greater stability at the ankle joint for weight-bearing in the erect position. On the other hand, the unusual medial extension of the articular surface of the head of the talus suggested a considerable mobility of the front part of the foot. Clearly, however, these inferences needed to be confirmed by more adequate material of the foot skeleton. Fortunately an australopithecine foot skeleton—almost complete except for the phalanges, the distal ends of the metatarsal bones, and the posterior part of the calcaneus—has been found at Olduvai in close association with the australopithecine jaw provisionally called "*pre-Zinjanthropus*" by Leakey (see Fig. 22). In this particular specimen the metatarsal of the great toe, though stoutly built, is not divergent (as shown by the presence at its base of an articular facet for the second metatarsal); on the other hand, the inclination of the upper articular facet of the talus indicates a mode of weight transmission to the foot that is not entirely like that of modern man (40).

Australopithecine hand bones from Olduvai have been described by Napier (97). The proximal and middle phalanges show evidence of powerful flexor muscles, while the terminal phalanges (in particular that of the thumb) "are characteristically *sapiens* in form." The carpal bones are, in general, similar to those of *Homo* (for example, the trapezium has a very well defined saddle-shaped surface), but in certain features they show resem-

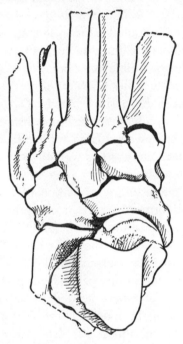

FIG. 22.—Dorsal view of the foot skeleton of one of the australopithecines found at Olduvai in Tanganyika. The front ends of the metatarsals and the back part of the calcaneus are missing. Approximately three-quarters natural size. (From a photograph kindly supplied by Dr. M. H. Day and Dr. J. R. Napier.)

blances to those of a juvenile gorilla. Napier remarks that "while morphologically the precise affinities of the Olduvai hand are indistinct, functionally there seems little reason to doubt that the hand is that of a hominid." The same author has also studied two metacarpal bones found in association with australopithecine remains at Swartkrans in South Africa. One of these (a thumb metacarpal) is exceptionally robust, "capable of great power and prehensile ability"; the other (a fourth metacarpal) is of much slighter construction and closely resembles that of *H. sapiens*. The elements of the upper-limb skeleton so far discovered and described are also consistent with the inference of erect bipedalism; for, again taken in combination, they conform closely in many details to the corresponding parts of the upper-limb skeleton of *Homo* and differ in several respects from those of the powerfully developed limbs of Recent anthropoid apes (80, 96, 97). They certainly do not show the pattern of characters which may be regarded as distinctive of upper limbs used either for quadrupedal progression or for a specialized type of brachiation.

So far as the posture is concerned, it will be observed that the evidence of the pelvis is confirmed by the other limb bones, and the evidence of the limb skeleton altogether is confirmed by morphological features of the skull. In other words, all the anatomical evidence is quite consistent within itself. That is to say, it indicates an erect posture and gait less efficient functionally than in modern man, but certainly hominid, and not pongid, in character. It is interesting to note that it is also consistent with the climatological evidence, for, as already pointed out, this indicates that the Australopithecinae were able to live in areas of comparative aridity. It seems certain, therefore, that they must have been well adapted to life in open terrain of the sort which still exists in the veldt lands of today.

Comparative studies by Dr. J. R. Napier and his colleagues suggest that, if all the limb-bones found in australopithecine deposits belong to the same or closely allied groups of hominids (and it would surely strain credulity beyond all reasonableness were this not so), the foot skeleton of the Australopithecinae approximated more closely to that of *Homo* than the hand skeleton. For while the former is almost as well adapted for erect bipedalism as in *Homo*, the latter indicates the possession of a "power grip" capable of fabricating crude stone implements but less certainly of a "precision grip" required for more delicate manipulations. Such a "mosaic" type of evolution in the early hominids, however, is perhaps to be expected, for only when erect bipedalism had become functionally well established would

165

the upper limb be completely freed to develop the morphological refinements characteristic of *Homo*.

4. The Taxonomic Status of the Australopithecinae

In chapter iii a provisional definition of the Hominidae was formulated on the basis of the known representatives of the genus *Homo*, that is, *H. sapiens*, *H. neanderthalensis*, and *H. erectus*. According to this definition, it is now clear that, as between the Pongidae and Hominidae, the Australopithecinae must be allocated to the latter family. They show none of the divergent modifications which are distinctive of the Pongidae, their only resemblances to the latter being the retention in common with them of primitive hominoid characters, such as the small size of the brain, large molar teeth, and certain rather minor features of the limb skeleton. As already discussed in detail, such primitive features must presumably have been present in the earlier phases of hominid evolution (as, indeed, they still were to some extent in *H. erectus*). The only other possible interpretation is that the Australopithecinae represent a third (and hitherto unknown) radiation of the Hominoidea with no particular relationship either to the Hominidae or the Pongidae, but showing a most extraordinary parallelism with the former. But such an interpretation would be wholly gratuitous, with no supporting evidence, and it would demand a degree of evolutionary parallelism far beyond anything that has been demonstrated to have occurred in any other mammalian sequence of evolution.

The recognition that the Australopithecinae belong to the hominid sequence of evolution does not necessarily mean, of course, that they were ancestral to the hominid species *H. erectus* and *H. sapiens*. Certainly, this is unlikely to have been the case with the South African fossils so far discovered; for it now seems probable that these particular individuals existed too late in geological time—at a time, indeed, when *H. erectus* was probably already living in the Far East. On the other hand, the greater antiquity of the Olduvai fossils suggests that the australopithecines of East Africa may have been the evolutionary precursors of *Homo* though it remains possible that some still earlier representatives of the Australopithecinae (perhaps in another part of the world) may have provided the ancestral basis from which all later hominids were derived. On purely morphological grounds there seems to be no serious objection to this interpretation, for in their skeletal and dental anatomy the Australopithecinae conform very closely indeed to theoretical postulates for a phase of hominid evolution immediately preceding the *H. erectus* phase. It is true that certain of their morphological features, such as the relatively large size of the premolars and molars and the degree of molarization of the first deciduous molar, have been interpreted as "specializations," with the implication that, not being present in later hominids, they could not have been present in the ancestors of the latter. In fact, however, there seems to be no sound basis for such a line of argument, for the so-called "specializations" are of such a minor character that their elimination in the course of subsequent evolutionary development may be quite easily postulated without doing violence to any known genetic or evolutionary principles (see p. 43).

We have been using the term "Australopithecinae" in reference to the whole collection of South African and East African fossils as a temporary device, in order to avoid confusion while the taxonomic nomenclature of the various groups still remains a matter of disagreement. And, as previously noted, the view taken here is that such anatomical differences as there may be between the fossil remains found at the different sites in the Transvaal (e.g., Taung, Sterkfontein, Kromdraai, Swartkrans, and Makapansgat) and in East Africa, though they may possibly justify subspecific, or even specific, distinctions, are not sufficient to justify generic distinctions. That is to say, the differences do not appear to equate in degree with those which are usually regarded as an adequate basis for generic distinctions in other groups of the Hominoidea. But the problem of the taxonomy of the Australopithecinae is basically a matter of the definition of terms; and until this has been attempted, it is hardly possible to achieve final agreement. On the assumption that all the australopithecine remains so far discovered represent a single genus only, *Australo-*

pithecus, this genus may be formally (and provisionally) defined as follows.

Australopithecus—a genus of the Hominidae distinguished by the following characters: relatively small cranial capacity, ranging from about 450 to well over 600 cc.; strongly built supra-orbital ridges; a tendency in individuals of larger varieties for the formation of a low sagittal crest in the frontoparietal region of the vertex of the skull (but not associated with a high nuchal crest); occipital condyles well behind the mid-point of the cranial length but on a transverse level with the auditory apertures; nuchal area of occiput restricted, as in *Homo;* consistent development (in immature as well as mature skulls) of a pyramidal mastoid process of typical hominid form and relationships; mandibular fossa constructed on the hominid pattern but in some individuals showing a pronounced development of the postglenoid process; massive jaws, showing considerable individual variation in respect of absolute size; mental eminence absent or slightly indicated; symphysial surface relatively straight and approaching the vertical; dental arcade parabolic in form with no diastema; spatulate canines wearing down flat from the tip only; relatively large premolars and molars; anterior lower premolar bicuspid with subequal cusps; pronounced molarization of first deciduous molar; progressive increase in size of permanent lower molars from first to third; the limb skeleton (so far as it is known) conforming in its main features to the hominid type but differing from *Homo* in a number of details, such as the forward prolongation of the region of the anterior superior spine of the ilium and a relatively small sacroiliac surface, the relatively low position (in some individuals) of the ischial tuberosity, and the marked forward prolongation of the intercondylar notch of the femur.

If this formal diagnosis of the genus *Australopithecus* is accepted, applying as it does to all the australopithecine material so far reported from the African continent, the question still remains whether this material justifies a subdivision of the genus in terms of species or subspecies. There is, of course, no doubt that there are certain morphological differences between the fossil individuals found at the different sites, and these permit a broad subdivision with two main groups. Those found at Krom-draai, Swartkrans, and Olduvai (i.e., *"Zinjanthropus"*) appear to be larger, with more massively constructed skulls, larger jaws and teeth, and a somewhat greater cranial capacity than those recovered from Taung, Sterkfontein, and Makapansgat. In the latter the typical australopithecine characters are less extremely developed; but whether these differences are adequate for a specific distinction is a question not easy to answer. Robinson (116) maintains that the two groups are generically distinct, and, because of his intimate acquaintance with most of the original material, his opinion deserves close consideration. But it has also been suggested that they bear a relation to one another which is comparable with that between the pygmy and other races of modern *H. sapiens;* if this latter analogy is strictly appropriate, there can hardly be any justification for according them even a specific distinction. Oakley advocates the recognition of two species of *Australopithecus,* an earlier *A. africanus* and a later *A. robustus.* As a provisional taxonomic device for distinguishing the two main groups, this is perhaps a reasonable compromise. Of these two types the former was smaller, lighter in build, and more slender in skeletal structure; the latter was a larger creature, more heavily built with a coarser skeletal structure, and showed a pronounced development of bony ridges and crests on the skull. On the basis of such differences it has been suggested that *A. africanus* is a more "advanced" type than *A. robustus,* but it seems more reasonable to regard it as a more generalized type of the same genus and thus more likely to have provided the ancestral basis for the subsequent evolution of *Homo.* If this interpretation is correct, it is to be assumed that *A. robustus* was a specialized type, somewhat divergent from the main line of hominid evolution. Further, if there were more or less contemporaneous and already distinct species in the African continent during early Pleistocene times, it follows that the divergence of the two types must have occurred earlier, perhaps in the late Pliocene. The foot skeleton found at Olduvai, approximating in its structure so closely to that of *Homo,* is no doubt one of the factors which has tempted the suggestion that a more "advanced" hominid genus

169

coexisted with *Australopithecus* in Africa. But it was found in close association with a mandible and lower dentition very characteristic of *A. africanus,* and there seems little reason to doubt that it is also attributable to this australopithecine species. Except for fragmentary remains, the foot skeleton of *A. robustus* is not known, but (as already noted) the lower extremities of the tibia and fibula found at Olduvai in association with *"Zinjanthropus"* (= *A. robustus*) indicates that, at least in the region of the ankle joint, the foot of this type of australopithecine was also well adapted for erect bipedalism.

There remains the difficult problem of the status of *"Telanthropus."* As already mentioned, this generic name was first given by Broom and Robinson to two mandibular specimens found at Swartkrans, in which the molar teeth (the only teeth preserved) are considerably smaller than other specimens found at the same site (though they are stated to "show general agreement in structure") and the mandible of lighter construction. A fragmentary specimen of a palate found at Swartkrans in 1952 was referred by Robinson (115) to the same genus. Broom and Robinson described these specimens as "human" or "euhominid," without, however, defining what they mean by these terms. On the other hand, Robinson specifically states that *"Telanthropus"* shows "australopithecine affinities." So far as it is possible to judge from diagrams and photographs, the *"Telanthropus"* specimens appear to harmonize quite closely in size and other features with the australopithecine maxilla found at Sterkfontein in 1936, and it appears doubtful, therefore, whether a generic distinction is warranted. They may indicate no more than a range of variation in size equivalent to that found in other hominoid genera; and, if this is so, they are no doubt of particular interest as demonstrating a range which overlaps with the megadont varieties of *H. erectus* and with *H. sapiens.* But, in any case, it will probably be agreed that more material needs to be collected before this question can be finally settled.

That the genus *Australopithecus* may have extended considerably beyond the limits of Africa was suggested by the illuminating comparisons which Robinson (114) made with the teeth and jaw fragments attributed by other workers to *"Meganthropus."* As already mentioned (p. 93), this term was first applied by von Koenigswald to the fragment of a large mandible found at Sangiran in Java in 1941. Apart from the remarkably close similarity of over-all dimensions (which, however, Robinson rightly regards as characters of very low phyletic valency), he demonstrated a most remarkable coincidence of cusp pattern between the first lower molar of the Javanese fossil and that of an australopithecine mandible found at Kromdraai. He further showed that the two upper premolars and an isolated upper molar discovered in East Africa by Kohl-Larsen in 1939, and referred by Weinert (161) and Remane (111) also to *"Meganthropus,"* are almost identical with the corresponding australopithecine teeth from South Africa. So far as these details of dental morphology are concerned, Robinson's inference that the *"Meganthropus"* specimens from Java and Africa may represent a once widely spread australopithecine group is not without good reason; but, here again, more adequate material (particularly of the skull) is required before such a conclusion can be substantiated. We have already noted (p. 94) that it does not seem feasible, on the basis of a small fragment of one mandible with only three teeth *in situ,* to differentiate *"Meganthropus"* from *H. erectus.*

Practically nothing is known of the activities or mode of life of *Australopithecus.* Attempts have been made to credit these creatures with the ability to use bone implements and even with the ability to make fire, but the evidence for the latter assumption has proved to be faulty. On the other hand, the fact that stone implements have been found in association with australopithecine remains at a number of different sites establishes a strong probability, and indeed a reasonable certainty, that they were tool-making creatures. Another indication that the Australopithecinae may have used weapons of some sort is provided by a large number of baboon (*Parapapio*) skulls which have been found associated with their remains, for (according to Barbour, 5), out of fifty-eight of these skulls, no less than forty-two (72 per cent) show evidence of depressed fractures in the parietal region which are rather consistent in position and extent. It has been suggested

171

that these injuries must have been the result of well-aimed blows with an implement of some sort, and it is certainly rather difficult to offer a more likely explanation. Thus, it now appears well assured that the Australopithecinae were endowed with an intelligence and skill superior to that of the modern anthropoid apes.

5. GENERAL OBSERVATIONS ON THE AUSTRALOPITHECINAE

The australopithecine fossils have been discussed in some detail because of their great importance for the study of human phylogeny. The remarkable quantity of the material so far discovered has already provided an unusual amount of information regarding the anatomical structure of these extinct creatures, but its very abundance means that its detailed analysis can be completed only after some years of study. It is clear, however, that the total morphological pattern presented by the skull, teeth, and postcranial skeleton conforms to that of the Hominidae rather than the Pongidae, in spite of the small size of the brain. But, while they are certainly hominids in the taxonomic sense, the terms "man" and "human" can only be applied to them with some reserve, for there is no certain evidence that they possessed any of the special attributes which are commonly associated with the human beings of today. They are to be regarded, rather, as representatives of the prehuman phase of the hominid sequence of evolution (85). In their morphology they appear to conform very closely to theoretical postulates for the immediate evolutionary precursors of the *H. erectus* (*Pithecanthropus*) phase of hominid evolution; and it is for this reason that the genus *Australopithecus* has been provisionally suggested as the ancestral stock (or at least very closely related to the ancestral stock) from which more advanced species of the Hominidae were derived. However, this interpretation depends on the demonstration that the genus actually does fit into the postulated *temporal* sequence. We have noted the evidence that some of the South African fossils prob- ably date from the Villafranchian period, and it has been esti- mated, on the basis of potassium-argon datings, that australo- pithecines inhabited East Africa well over a million years ago. Thus, there is no theoretical difficulty (from the point of view of the geological sequence) in accepting *Australopithecus* as ancestral to *H. erectus* and *H. sapiens*. Even so, however, it would not necessarily follow that the transition occurred in Africa. It may have occurred in some other part of the world, and the African fossils in that case may represent but slightly modified survivors of the ancestral stock, which persisted to a much later time in the Transvaal. It should be noted that remains attributed by some authorities to the Australopithecinae have been found near Lake Eyasi in Tanganyika, near Lake Tchad (32), and in the Jordan Valley (138), the last being associated with pebble tools similar to those found with the australopithecine skull at Olduvai. The similarity of the molar teeth of the Javanese fossil *"Meganthropus"* (as we have noted) has also led Robinson to conclude that this is still another representative of the Australopithecinae (114). It would seem prudent, however, to defer acceptance of these identifications until more complete material comes to light. If the identifications should prove correct, they would indicate a very wide geographical distribution of the australopithecines in the early Pleistocene. Obviously, the precise position of *Australopithecus* in hominid phylogeny can be determined only by a more complete paleontological record. But it may be emphasized that, even if evidence of geological antiquity were totally lacking, the purely morphological evidence of the Australopithecinae would still be highly significant. For they demonstrate (what had already been predicated from a consideration of comparative anatomical data and of the paleoanthropological sequence leading back to *H. erectus*) that there once existed primitive hominids with a cranial capacity exceeding by very little that of the large anthropoid apes but with a limb structure evidently related to the development of an erect posture and gait which is so marked a characteristic of the evolutionary sequence of the Hominidae in general.

CHAPTER V

The Origin of the Hominidae

Undoubtedly the most intriguing question in the whole evolutionary story is, What was the ultimate origin of man? Or, put in zoölogical phraseology, at what stage in geological time did the Hominidae become finally segregated from other groups of the Primates, and what was the nature of the ancestral stock from which this segregation occurred? Unfortunately, any answers which can at present be given to these questions are based on indirect evidence and thus are largely conjectural, for the paleontological record of the Hominidae is still incomplete. The gradational series of types—modern *Homo sapiens,* Early Mousterian and Acheulian man, *Homo erectus* (*Pithecanthropus*), and *Australopithecus*—comprise a retrospective sequence morphologically, and also (now that *Australopithecus* has been shown to have existed in the initial phases of the Villafranchian period) a receding temporal sequence (Fig. 23). They would thus seem to provide satisfactory evidence for carrying our ancestral lineage back to a phase of hominid evolution to which the term "human" can hardly any longer be applied—when the size of the brain was little greater than that of the modern anthropoid apes and the jaws were massive and protruding. But it is a phase which still appears (in spite of the small brain) to have been well advanced beyond the initial origin of the Hominidae, that is to say, long after the time of their evolutionary segregation from the Pongidae. For example, many characteristic features of the hominid skull and dentition had already been established by what may be termed the "*Australopithecus* phase," and (what is still more important) the limb skeleton had already undergone a considerable degree of modification in adaptation to an erect posture and gait, very different indeed from that which must be postulated, on the basis of comparative anatomical evidence, for a common ancestral stock. The fact is that the most serious hiatus now in the record of hominid evolution is the gap which separates the genus *Australopithecus* from the fossil hominoids of Pliocene and Miocene times. It is true that, by extrapolation backward and by analogy with what is known of the paleontological history of other mammalian groups, we can contrive a theoretical picture of the intermediate stages which presumably must have been interposed between generalized pongid ancestors and the *Australopithecus* phase; but, in the absence of the concrete evidence of fossil remains, this is not a very satisfying procedure.

So far, no fossil remains generally accepted as hominids have been found in geological deposits which can with any certainty be assigned to an antiquity greater than the Early Pleistocene. Nor have any artificially fabricated implements been convincingly shown to be of earlier date (in spite of the prolonged controversy in the past on "eoliths"). Pliocene hominids have been postulated, and it is certain that they existed, but, with the possible exception of *Ramapithecus* (see p. 178), their relics have yet to be discovered. On the other hand, fossilized remains of anthropoid apes have been found in Pliocene and Miocene deposits over wide areas of the Old World. It is worth giving brief consideration to these, since they represent, so to speak, the other side of the gap in the paleontological record of the Hominidae.

More than twenty different genera of large extinct hominoids of Pliocene or Miocene age have been described from sites in Europe, India, and Africa (79, 81), but critical studies in recent years indicate fairly clearly that these fossils represent at most only four distinct genera, i.e., *Dryopithecus, Sivapithecus, Proconsul,* and *Ramapithecus,* and, apart from *Ramapithecus* even these may warrant no more than a subgeneric distinction. Only the skull of *Proconsul* is known from almost complete specimens. As may be seen in Fig. 24, this skull is of a generalized type, with no more than a moderate prognathism and lacking the supra-orbital torus and high nuchal crest of the modern African apes. It is to be noted, however, that this is an isolated example of a small and lightly built creature and may not therefore be assumed to be typical

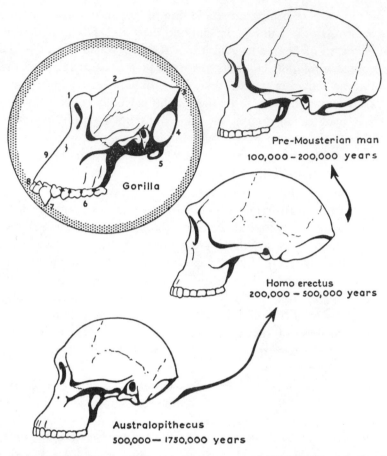

Pre-Mousterian man
100,000 - 200,000 years

Homo erectus
200,000 - 500,000 years

Australopithecus
500,000 - 1750,000 years

Gorilla

FIG. 23.—This diagram illustrates the appearance of the skull in a series of fossil hominid types arranged in their temporal sequence. The antiquity of each type has been estimated by methods of relative or absolute dating, but should be regarded as no more than approximate within very broad limits. It is also to be noted that some of these types overlapped in time in different geographical regions. The representation of the genus *Australopithecus* is based on a skull found at Sterkfontein in South Africa, *Homo erectus* on a skull cap and portions of jaws found in Java, pre-Mousterian man on the Steinheim skull, early Mousterian man on one of the skulls found at Mount Carmel in Palestine, and Neanderthal man on a skull found at Monte Circeo in Italy. Inset on the left is shown, for comparison and contrast, the skull of an adult female gorilla; the numerals indicate a few of the fundamental characters which, taken in combination, comprise a total morphological pattern distin-

176

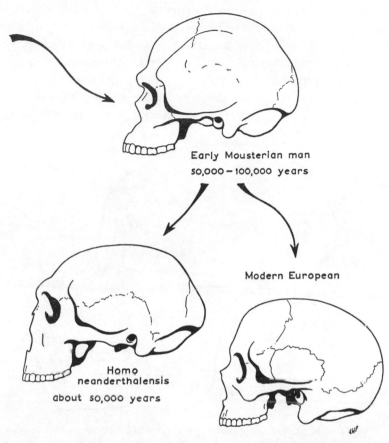

Early Mousterian man
50,000 – 100,000 years

Modern European

Homo
neanderthalensis
about 50,000 years

guishing the anthropoid ape type of skull from the hominid type of skull. The characters indicated are: (*1*) The forward projection of the brow ridges well beyond the front end of the brain-case; (*2*) The low level of the cranial roof in relation to the upper border of the orbital aperture; (*3*) The high position of the external occipital protuberance; (*4*) The steep slope and great extent of the nuchal area of the occiput for the attachment of the neck muscles; (*5*) The relatively backward position of the occipital condyles; (*6*) Except in advanced stages of attrition the teeth are not worn down to a flat, even surface; (*7*) The canines form conical, projecting, and sharply pointed "tusks"; (*8*) The large size of the incisor teeth; (*9*) The massive upper jaw. Note, also, that in the hominid type of skull a pyramidal mastoid process of quite distinctive pattern is consistently present. All the skulls have been drawn to the same scale. (From the Proc. Amer. Phil. Soc., **103,** 1959.)

of Miocene and Pliocene apes in general. In most cases Miocene and Pliocene hominoids are known only from jaws and teeth, the former usually being very fragmentary. In the majority of specimens the dentition conforms in its general features to the pongid type, with projecting and conical canines, sectorial lower first premolars, and elongated molars which are usually large and, in the lower dentition, increase progressively in size from front to

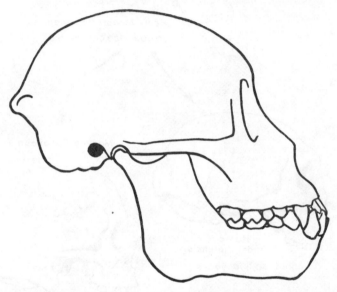

Fig. 24.—The skull of the Miocene ape, *Proconsul africanus*, as reconstructed by Davis and Napier (39).

back. On the other hand, the cusp pattern of the molars can be distinguished from that of the modern large apes and is, in general, less complicated: the incisor teeth are relatively smaller (and in this respect more closely resemble hominid incisors), and the simian shelf of the mandible is either absent or developed only in an incipient form. In other words, the dentition and mandible of these early hominoids were less specialized than in Recent Pongidae. Of special importance is the Pliocene hominoid described by Gregory, Hellman, and Lewis (48) from the Siwalik deposits of India, *Ramapithecus*, which, in the small size of the teeth and the relatively simple construction of the molars, seems to approximate more closely to the Hominidae than do the other hominoid genera. The somewhat flattened wear of the premolars and molars, the bicuspid character of the former, the small size of the canines (as judged by their sockets), the orientation of the long axes of their alveoli and their medial position in the lower dentition, the moderate degree of anterior convergence of the tooth rows in the maxilla to form a parabolic dental arcade (Fig. 25), the absence of a pronounced diastema, and the relatively low degree of prognathism are all rather suggestive of the sort of transitional phase which may be presumed to have occurred in the evolutionary derivation of the hominid type of dentition from that characteristic of known Pliocene and Miocene apes. Indeed, Simons inclines to the view that the total morphological pattern provided by these features in combination indicates that the genus should be more properly allocated to the Hominidae than to the Pongidae (129). In this connection it is perhaps significant that the remains of *Ramapithecus* were recovered from the Nagri zone of the Siwalik formations, which (according to Colbert's data, 28) corresponds to the Lower or Early Middle Pliocene. That is to say, it is one of the latest representatives of the extinct hominoids which were so widely dispersed during the Miocene and Pliocene. Unfortunately, the relevant fossil material from India is still too scanty to permit any definite formulation of an evolutionary sequence adumbrating the initial segregation of the Hominidae, even though the indications provided by the few Siwalik specimens already obtained are sufficiently interesting to arouse the hope that this region will sometime be systematically and carefully explored for further evidence in this direction. It certainly does seem to offer rich prospects for the paleoanthropologist. But it is possible that the pertinent evidence may eventually be forthcoming from East Africa, for a maxilla of *Ramapithecus* with much of the upper dentition has been discovered by Leakey at Fort Ternan in Kenya from deposits of approximately the same geological age as those which yielded the *Ramapithecus* maxilla in India. Leakey named his specimen *Kenyapithecus* on the basis of certain trivial differences from the Indian specimen, but, as Simons has noted, "greater differences than have been noted here typically occur among members of a single family social group within nearly all species of present day hominoids" (131).

Reference should be made here to the Pliocene ape *Oreopithecus,* of which jaws with the dentition were first described almost a hundred years ago. In more recent times much richer material of this fossil hominoid has been found in lignite deposits in Tuscany by Hürzeler (58), including an almost complete (but badly crushed) skeleton. In a number of characters *Oreopithecus* does show an approximation to the Hominidae, for example, in the small size of the canine tooth, the bicuspid character of the front

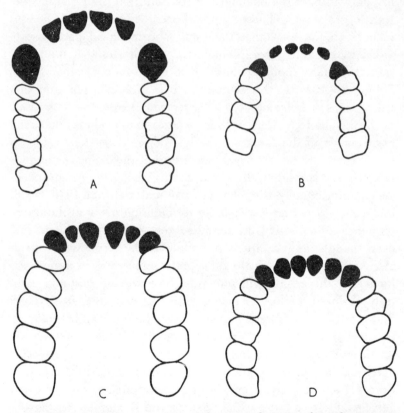

Fɪɢ. 25.—Palatal view in outline of the upper dentition of A, Chimpanzee; B, *Ramapithecus;* C, *Australopithecus;* and D, an Australian aboriginal. Approximately natural size. In all cases the incisors and canines are represented by their sockets only. The sockets in *Ramapithecus* have been in part reconstructed.

lower premolar, the vertical symphysis of the mandible, and the breadth of the iliac bone. On the other hand, the lower molar teeth display certain cercopithecoid traits (particularly in the elongated talonid of the third molar), the increased breadth of the iliac bone involves its anterior region (and not, as in the hominid pelvis, the posterior region), and the relative elongation of the upper limbs clearly indicates an advanced degree of specialized brachiation quite similar to that of the modern anthropoid apes. There is now general agreement that while *Oreopithecus* is certainly a hominoid (and not, as at one time supposed, a deviant type of cercopithecoid), the genus must be regarded taxonomically as a somewhat aberrant pongid retaining a few residual cercopithecoid characters. Hürzeler's suggestion that it is a primitive hominid having a place in the direct ancestry of man has not been found acceptable.

The question now arises whether there is any theoretical objection to postulating the derivation of the hominid type of dentition from the pongid type of dentition represented in the known Miocene apes of generalized type such as *Dryopithecus*. It has indeed been argued that the projecting conical canines and the sectorialized lower first premolars found in these apes (wherein they approximate closely to the modern apes) are specializations which could not have found a place in hominid ancestry. But this line of argument appears to be based on quite arbitrary assumptions as to what should be regarded as "specializations," and also on the false premise that even a slight degree of morphological specialization is not capable of undergoing an evolutionary reversal (see p. 43). So far as the canine tooth is concerned, it is first to be observed that in the Miocene and Pliocene genera of hominoids it actually showed a good deal of variation in size; we have already noted that in *Ramapithecus* it was an unusually small tooth. Second, there is reasonably good evidence of a direct anatomical nature that the small, spatulate canine of *H. sapiens* is the result of a secondary reduction in size. For example, the newly erupted and unworn canine (particularly the deciduous canine) may project quite markedly beyond the level of the adjacent teeth and may occasionally also be sharply pointed. Again, the permanent canine is provided with an unusually robust root, and the latter is also longer than that of the immediately adjacent teeth (Fig. 26); such features are difficult to explain on a purely functional basis, for in modern man the canines have no special function to perform. But they do become intelligible if we suppose that they had special functions in the past. Finally, the eruption of the permanent canine in *H. sapiens* is still late relatively to the eruption of the adjacent teeth; it may come into place only after the two premolars and sometimes even after the second molar. There is also the evidence of fossil hominids that the modern canine has

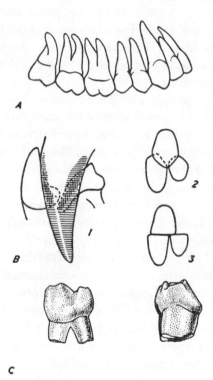

Fig. 26.—Diagram illustrating *A*, the relatively long and robust root of the upper canine tooth in *Homo sapiens; B*, the occlusal relationships of the canines and a sectorial first lower premolar tooth in a cercopithecoid monkey (*1*), and the occlusal relationship of the canines and the first lower premolar tooth in *Homo sapiens* before attrition (*2*), and at an early stage of attrition (*3*) (after Remane); and *C*, lateral and anterior views of a first lower milk molar tooth of *Homo sapiens*.

undergone retrogressive modifications, for (as we have noted, p. 101) in *Homo erectus* (*Pithecanthropus*) the canines in some individuals were relatively large, overlapping teeth, associated with a definite diastema.

That the sectorial and predominantly unicuspid first lower premolar tooth (except in its extreme form) is really a primitive and not a specialized feature of the hominoid dentition and that the bicuspid hominid tooth is secondarily derived are indicated by a number of considerations. In the first place, the sectorial type of tooth is a functional correlate of a projecting and overlapping upper canine, for it is shaped in conformity with the occlusal requirements of the latter. Second, in every genus of the earlier fossil Hominoidea so far known (even as far back as the little *Parapithecus* of Oligocene times), the first lower premolar is a predominantly unicuspid tooth,[1] and, indeed, this is a character of the primitive mammalian dentition as a whole. The evolutionary derivation of a bicuspid premolar from a unicuspid tooth is, after all, only one example of the tendency for an elaboration ("molarization") of the premolars which is a quite common feature in the phylogenesis of other groups of Primates. Lastly, as Remane (110) has pointed out, in *H. sapiens* the morphology of the first deciduous molar, i.e., the temporary precursor of the first lower premolar, offers very suggestive evidence, for it is often quite markedly compressed from side to side, with the anterolateral surface sloping obliquely downward, very much as that of a sectorial tooth does (Fig. 26). It is not improbable that this feature is an example of the astonishing conservatism of morphological elements, as the result of which form and structure may persist for a long geological time after they have ceased to serve their original function.

These, then, are the lines of evidence which lead to the inference that the bicuspid premolar of hominid type is secondarily derived from a predominantly unicuspid and (moderately) sectorial tooth not very dissimilar to that still found in the modern

---

[1] The statement has been made that, in the primitive hominoid mandibles of Oligocene date, the first lower premolar has a bicuspid form of hominid type. This, however, is not the case.

large apes.[2] And it is to be noted that the inference accords well with the evidence that the brachydont hominid canine is a secondary modification of a conical, projecting canine. It hardly needs to be emphasized again that the final proof of such an evolutionary sequence must depend on adequate paleontological documentation; but it is at least clear that there is no theoretical reason why the hominid type of dentition should not have been derived from the generalized pongid type found in some of the Miocene or Pliocene apes, and such indirect evidence as is available certainly supports this proposition.

Apart from the dentition, it seems that some authorities have been reluctant to accept the suggestion that the evolutionary precursors of the Hominidae could be represented by any of the known Miocene or Pliocene genera of apes, on the assumption that, because their dental characters show quite definitely that most of them were certainly pongids, they must therefore have shown aberrant specializations in limb structure, etc., comparable with those characteristic of the modern anthropoid apes. In fact, however, there has never been any real basis for such an assumption; on the contrary, by analogy with what is now known of the evolution of other mammalian groups, it might have been anticipated that the limb structure of these extinct hominoids would still have preserved a much more generalized condition—approximating in some degree, that is to say, to that of the quadrupedal cercopithecoid monkeys. Paleontological discovery has shown that this certainly was the case, at least with some of the extinct genera. From Pliocene and Miocene deposits of Europe a femur[3] and the shaft of a humerus of *Dryopithecus* are known and also, from the Miocene, the skeleton of a small gibbon-like ape,

[2] It has already been noted (p. 108) that in the genus *Homo* the lingual cusp of the first lower premolar (which is so conspicuous in more primitive hominids) has undergone a secondary reduction.

[3] This femur was discovered over a hundred years ago, and for many years it was assumed to be that of a giant gibbon. But no remains of a giant gibbon have ever been found in Europe (or, for that matter, elsewhere). The femur is certainly a pongid femur of some sort, and the only large Pongidae known to have existed contemporaneously in Europe are the dryopithecine apes. The femur conforms very well to the probable size of these apes, and there can therefore be little doubt that it must be referred to *Dryopithecus*.

Pliopithecus (41, 165). Relatively complete, but rather fragmentary, remains of the limb skeleton of Miocene apes have been recovered from East Africa. Taken all together, this evidence indicates that the limb structure of these extinct apes had certainly not developed the extreme and aberrant specializations of the modern anthropoid apes. The shafts of the dryopithecine humerus and femur are slender and straight and suggest lightly built and agile creatures. The limb bones of *Pliopithecus* recently found in Middle Miocene deposits in Austria are, according to a most detailed study by Zapfe (165), quite astonishingly primitive in their general construction and, in some of their morphological details, resemble those of cercopithecoid type. The humerus and femur of the Early Miocene genus *Proconsul* from East Africa are quite similar to those of *Dryopithecus*, and the calcaneus and talus show interesting differences from those of the modern apes (86). In another East African Miocene pongid, *Limnopithecus*, which is evidently an extinct representative of the Hylobatinae (and perhaps not really generically distinct from *Pliopithecus*), the limb skeleton, in its proportions and morphological details, also shows a number of cercopithecoid characters (87). So far as it goes, then, the paleontological evidence suggests that in their limb structure at least some, and perhaps all, of the Miocene and Pliocene apes had not at that time developed the specializations related to the extreme form of brachiation shown by the modern apes, which is associated with characteristic changes in limb proportions. On the contrary, they were evidently in some ways more like the quadrupedal cercopithecoid monkeys of today, active and agile creatures, capable of scampering on the ground as well as leaping among the branches of the trees. The importance of these observations is clear, for they demonstrate that, so far as the proportions and structural adaptations of the limbs are concerned, there appears now to be no theoretical objection to the derivation of the Hominidae and the Recent Pongidae from a common ancestry at least as late as Early or Middle Miocene times, and possibly even later. It was perhaps subsequent to this time, therefore, that, in association with opposing trends in adaptation to posture and gait, the divergent evolutionary development of characteristic growth rates of the limb and trunk in the Hominoidea marked the initial phylogenetic separation of the earliest precursors of the Hominidae from the Pongidae.

It has been argued that, since the terms "anthropoid ape" and "pongid" were originally defined by reference to the modern anthropoid apes, which are characterized by certain specializations in limb proportions, etc., they can hardly be applied to extinct genera in which (as is now known) these specializations were not fully developed. But this seems to be taking too static and narrow a view of the definition of larger taxonomic categories. In the case of the Miocene apes, their inclusion in the Pongidae appears valid for the following reasons: (1) a major taxonomic category should naturally include not only the terminal products of its evolution but also the earlier phases of development through which it passed after it became definitely segregated from immediately related groups; (2) it is to be expected that the earlier representatives of the Pongidae, after their initial segregation from the Cercopithecoidea, would retain primitive characters which became lost in the course of later evolution; (3) there is good evidence that the Cercopithecoidea had, in fact, already become a separate and well-defined group by the Early Miocene, for fossil remains of a cercopithecoid monkey (provisionally identified as *Mesopithecus*) have been recovered from the Early Miocene deposits of East Africa showing the specialized dental features distinctive of the whole group; (4) the dental morphology of the Miocene apes approximates very closely to that of the Recent Pongidae, and in certain elements of the dentition (e.g., the canines and premolars) appears in some cases to be indistinguishable; (5) a difference in limb proportions does not by itself constitute an adequate basis for a familial distinction; (6) in spite of their general cercopithecoid appearance, the limb bones of some of the Miocene apes (e.g., *Limnopithecus*) do show certain features in which they approximate to the Recent Pongidae. If all these factors are given due consideration, it seems reasonable to include these extinct genera of fossil apes (so far as they are at present known) in the Pongidae, though it may perhaps be justifiable to accord them a subfamilial distinction.

186

The factors which determined the segregation of the evolutionary radiation of the Hominidae can be only conjectured. There is no reason to suppose that the Miocene and Pliocene apes were not arboreal creatures (even though it seems likely that they were also capable of active progression on the ground), but there existed in the Early Miocene of East Africa a large ape, *Proconsul major*, which was evidently equivalent in size to the modern gorilla (86); this creature must presumably have been restricted in its arboreal habits to the main branches of the trees at the lower levels near the ground and may even have been mainly terrestrial. It would be particularly interesting to know something of the limb structure of *P. major*, but, unfortunately, no limb bones have been found (except for some not very informative fragments of the clavicle). That the adoption of bipedal terrestrial habits by the earliest representatives of the Hominidae must have occurred in regions of deforestation seems very probable; and it is perhaps significant, therefore, that the environment of the East African Miocene apes provided possibilities of this sort. A consideration of fossilized fruits, seeds, and insects discovered by Dr. L. S. B. Leakey in the Miocene deposits of Kenya (as well as the evidence of the general faunal assemblage) indicates that this environment consisted of wooded valleys of limited extent, separated by open savanna country—there were probably no large continuous tracts of tropical forest comparable to those inhabited by the modern anthropoid apes. It may be suggested that the evolution of ground-living forms in the ancestry of the Hominidae was the result of adaptations primarily concerned, not with the abandonment of arboreal life, but (paradoxically) with an attempt to retain it. For in regions undergoing gradual deforestation they would make it possible to cross intervening grasslands in order to pass from one restricted and shrinking wooded area to another (85). This proposition is parallel to the interesting conjecture that water-living vertebrates initially acquired terrestrial and air-breathing adaptations in order to preserve their aquatic mode of life; for in times of drought these adaptations would make it possible to escape from dried-up rivers or pools and go overland in search of water elsewhere.

Those anatomists who have persuaded themselves of the "uniqueness" of man's anatomical structure have commonly assigned to him a vast geological antiquity. But, as already pointed out in the first chapter (p. 4), there is no objective reason for assuming that the family of the Hominidae, *morphologically speaking*, is more "unique" than any other family of the Mammalia. So far as the evidence at present available can be assessed, the origin of the Hominidae and the Pongidae from a common ancestral stock seems well assured. There is no sound argument for pushing back the origin of the Hominidae to the Oligocene (or, as some would even suggest, to the Eocene). There is, in fact, no reason why it may not have occurred in the early part of the Pliocene. It is here a question of attempting to estimate the time factor which is likely to have been involved in the evolutionary development of those characters which are distinctive of the Hominidae. But arguments based on the analogy of evolution rates in other mammalian groups are, unfortunately, far from secure.

The interpretation of the paleontological evidence of hominid evolution which has been offered in the preceding chapters is a provisional interpretation. Because of the incompleteness of the evidence, it could hardly be otherwise. But it is an interpretation which appears to accord reasonably well with the facts at present available. In one of his many writings, Karl Pearson made the observation, "Science consists not in absolute knowledge, but in the statement of the probable on the basis of our present—invariably limited—acquaintance with facts." To no branch of science can this be more aptly applied than to the science of paleoanthropology.

References

1. ARAMBOURG, C. 1957. Récentes découvertes de paléontologie humaine en Afrique du Nord française, Proc. Third Pan-African Congress on Prehistory, London, p. 186.
2. ARAMBOURG, C., and BIBERSON, P. 1955. Découvertes de vestiges humains acheuléens dans la carrière de Sidi Abd-er-Rahman. C.R. Acad. Sc., 240:1661.
3. ASHTON, E. H., and ZUCKERMAN, S. 1950. Some quantitative dental characters of fossil anthropoids, Phil. Tr. Roy. Soc., B, 234:485.
4. ——. 1951. Statistical methods in anthropology, Nature, 168: 1116.
5. BARBOUR, G. B. 1949. Ape or man? Ohio J. Sc., 49:4.
6. BATTAGLIA, R. 1948. Osso occipitale umano rinvenuto del giacimento Pleistocenico di quinzano del Commune di Verona, Palaeont. ital., 42:1.
7. BERGMAN, R. A. M., and KARSTEN, P. 1952. The fluorine content of Pithecanthropus and of other specimens from the Trinil fauna, Proc. Kon. Akad. Wetensch., Amsterdam, 55:151.
8. BLACK, D. 1930. On an adolescent skull of Sinanthropus pekinensis, Palaeont. Sinica, Ser. D, 7:1.
9. ——. 1933. On the endocranial cast of the adolescent Sinanthropus skull, Proc. Roy. Soc. London, B, 112:263.
10. BONIN, G. VON. 1928–30. Studien zum Homo rhodesiensis, Ztschr. f. Morphol. u. Anthropol., 2:347.
11. BOULE, M., and VALLOIS, H. V. Fossil Men. London: Thames and Hudson.
12. BRAIN, C. K. 1955. New evidence for the correlation of the Transvaal ape-man bearing deposits, Proc. Third Pan-African Congress on Prehistory, p. 143.
13. BRONOWSKI, J., and LONG, W. M. 1951. Statistical methods in anthropology, Nature, 168:794.
14. ——. 1952. Statistics of discrimination in anthropology, Am. J. Phys. Anthropol., 10:385.
15. ——. 1953. The australopithecine milk canines, Nature, 172:251.
16. BROOM, R., and ROBINSON, J. T. 1949. The lower end of the femur of Plesianthropus, Ann. Transvaal Mus., 21:181.
17. ——. 1950. Man contemporaneous with the Swartkrans ape-man, Am. J. Phys. Anthropol., 8:151.

18. BROOM, R., and ROBINSON, J. T. 1951. Eruption of the permanent teeth in the South African fossil ape-men, Nature, **167**:443.
19. ——. 1952. Swartkrans ape-man, *Paranthropus crassidens,* Transvaal Mus. Mem., No. 6.
20. BROOM, R.; ROBINSON, J. T.; and SCHEPERS, G. W. H. 1950. The Sterkfontein ape-man, *Plesianthropus,* Transvaal Mus. Mem., No. 4.
21. BROOM, R., and SCHEPERS, G. W. H. 1946. The South African fossil ape-men: the Australopithecinae, Transvaal Mus. Mem., No. 2.
22. BROTHWELL, D. R. 1961. The people of Mount Carmel, Proc. Prehist. Soc., **27**:155.
23. BRUMMELKAMP, R. 1940. On the cephalization stage of *Pithecanthropus erectus* and *Sinanthropus pekinensis,* Proc. Kon. Akad. Wetensch., Amsterdam, **43**:3.
24. BUXTON, L. H. D. 1938. Platymeria and Platycnemia, J. Anat., **73**:31.
25. BUXTON, L. H. D., and MORANT, G. M. 1933. The essential craniological technique, J. Roy. Anthropol. Inst., **63**:19.
26. CHANG, K. C. 1962. New evidence of fossil man in China, Science, **136**:749.
27. CLARK, J. DESMOND. 1950. New studies on Rhodesian man, J. Roy. Anthropol. Inst., **77**:13.
28. COLBERT, E. H. 1935. Siwalik mammals in the American Museum of Natural History, Tr. Am. Phil. Soc., **26**:1.
29. ——. 1949. Some palaeontological principles significant in human evolution. *In:* Early man in the Far East, p. 103. ("Studies in physical anthropology," No. 1.) Pub. by American Association of Physical Anthropology.
30. COOKE, H. B. S. 1952. Mammals, ape-men, and Stone Age men in southern Africa, South African Archeol. Bull., **7**:59.
31. COON, C. S. 1962. The Origin of Races. New York: A. A. Knopf.
32. COPPEN, Y. 1961. Découverte d'un Australopitheciné dans le Villafranchien du Tchad, C.R. Acad. Sc., **252**:3851.
33. DART, R. A. 1925. *Australopithecus africanus:* the man-ape of South Africa, Nature, **115**:195.
34. ——. 1948. The Makapansgat proto-human *Australopithecus prometheus,* Am. J. Phys. Anthropol., **6**:259.
35. ——. 1948. The adolescent mandible of *Australopithecus prometheus, ibid.,* p. 391.
36. ——. 1949. Innominate fragments of *Australopithecus prometheus, ibid.,* **7**:301.
37. ——. 1958. A further adolescent australopithecine ilium from Makapansgat, *ibid.,* **16**:473.

38. DAVIS, P. R. 1964. A tibia and fibula from Bed 1, Olduvai, Tanganyika, Nature, **201**:967.
39. DAVIS, P. R., and NAPIER, J. R. 1963. Reconstruction of the skull of *Proconsul africanus*, Folia Primatologica, **1**:20.
40. DAY, M. H., and NAPIER, J. R. 1963. The fossil foot from Olduvai gorge: a provisional report, Nature, **201**:967.
41. DEPÉRET, C. 1887. Études paléontologiques dans le Bassin du Rhône, Arch. Mus. Hist. Nat., Lyons, **4**:45.
42. DRENNAN, M. R., and SINGER, R. 1955. A mandibular fragment, probably of the Saldanha skull, Nature, **175**:364.
43. DUBOIS, E. 1932. The distinct organization of *Pithecanthropus erectus* now confirmed from other individuals of the described species, Proc. Kon. Akad. Wetensch., Amsterdam, **35**:716.
44. ELLIOT SMITH, G. 1931. The search for man's ancestors. London: Watts & Co.
45. FORD, E. B. 1938. The genetic basis of adaptation. *In:* G. R. DE BEER (ed.), Evolution, p. 43. London: Oxford University Press.
46. GORJANOVIĆ-KRAMBERGER, K. 1906. Der diluviale Mensch von Krapina in Kroatien. Wiesbaden: C. W. Kreidler.
47. GREGORY, W. K., and HELLMAN, M. 1923. Notes on the type of *Hesperopithecus haroldcookii*, Am. Mus. Novitiates, No. 53, p. 1.
48. GREGORY, W. K.; HELLMAN, M.; and LEWIS, C. E. 1938. Fossil anthropoids of the Yale-Cambridge Indian Expedition of 1935, "Carnegie Institution of Washington Publications," No. 495.
49. HALDANE, J. B. S. 1949. Suggestions as to quantitative measurement of rates of evolution, Evolution, **3**:51.
50. HAXTON, H. A. 1947. Muscles of the pelvic limb: a study of the differences between bipeds and quadrupeds, Anat. Rec., **98**:337.
51. HAY, R. L. 1963. Stratigraphy of Beds 1 through IV, Olduvai gorge, Tanganyika, Science, **139**:829.
52. HIGGS, E. 1961. Some Pleistocene faunas of the Mediterranean coastal areas, Proc. Prehist. Soc., **27**:144.
53. HIRSCHLER, P. 1942. Anthropoid and human endocranial casts. Amsterdam: N. V. Noord-Hollandsche Uitgevers Maatschappij.
54. HOOIJER, D. A. 1951. The geological ape of *Pithecanthropus, Meganthropus,* and *Gigantopithecus,* Am. J. Phys. Anthropol., **9**:265.
55. HOWELL, J. CLARK. 1951. The place of Neanderthal man in human evolution, Am. J. Phys. Anthropol., **9**:379.
56. ———. 1952. Pleistocene glacial ecology and the evolution of "classic Neanderthal" man, Southwestern J. Anthropol., **8**:377.
57. HRDLIČKA, A. 1930. The skeletal remains of early man, Smithsonian Misc. Coll., **83**:1.
58. HÜRZELER, J. 1958. *Oreopithecus bambolii,* Verhandl. Natur. Gesell. Basel, **69**:1.

59. KAPPERS, C. U. A. 1929. The fissures on the frontal lobes of *Pithecanthropus erectus,* Proc. Kon. Akad. Wetensch., Amsterdam, **32**:1.

60. KAPPERS, C. U. A., and BOUMAN, K. H. 1939. Comparison of the endocranial casts of the *Pithecanthropus erectus* skull found by Dubois and von Koenigswald's *Pithecanthropus* skull, Proc. III Cong. Neurol. Internat., Copenhagen.

61. KEITH, A. 1925. The antiquity of man. London: Williams & Norgate.

62. ———. 1931. Further discoveries relating to the antiquity of man. London: Williams & Norgate.

63. KERN, H. M., and STRAUS, W. L. 1949. The femur of *Plesianthropus transvaalensis,* Am. J. Phys. Anthropol., **7**:53.

64. KOENIGSWALD, G. H. R. VON. 1936. Erste Mitteilung ueber einen fossilen Hominiden aus dem Altpleistocän Ostjavas, Proc. Kon. Akad. Wetensch., Amsterdam, **39**:1.

65. ———. 1937. Ein Unterkieferfragment des *Pithecanthropus* aus den Trinilschichten Mitteljavas, *ibid.,* **40**:1.

66. ———. 1938. Ein neuer *Pithecanthropus*-Schaedel, *ibid.,* **41**:1.

67. ———. 1940. Neue *Pithecanthropus*-Funde 1936–1938, Wetensch. Meded., No. 28.

68. ———. 1949. The discovery of early man in Java and southern China. *In:* Early man in the Far East, p. 83. ("Studies in physical anthropology," No. 1.) Published by the American Association of Physical Anthropology.

69. ———. 1950. Fossil hominids from the Lower Pleistocene of Java, Proc. of 18th Internat. Geol. Cong., Part IX, p. 59.

70. ———. 1962. Das absolute Alter des *Pithecanthropus erectus.* in Evolution and Hominization. Ed. by G. Kurth. Stuttgart, p. 113.

71. KOENIGSWALD, G. H. R. VON, and WEIDENREICH, F. 1939. The relationship between *Pithecanthropus* and *Sinanthropus,* Nature, **144**:926.

72. LEAKEY, L. S. B. 1959. A new fossil skull from Olduvai, Nature, **184**:491.

73. ———. 1960. Recent discoveries at Olduvai gorge, *ibid.,* **188**: 1050.

74. ———. 1961. New finds at Olduvai gorge, *ibid.,* **189**:649.

75. ———. 1961. A new lower Pliocene fossil Primate from Kenya, Ann. Mag. Nat. Hist. Ser. 13, **4**:689.

76. LE GROS CLARK, W. E. 1928. Rhodesian man, Man, **28**:206.

77. ———. 1934. The asymmetry of the occipital region of the brain and skull, *ibid.,* **34**:1.

78. ———. 1938. General features of the Swanscombe skull bones and endocranial cast, J. Roy. Anthrop. Inst., **68**:58.

79. ———. 1940. Palaeontological evidence bearing on human evolution, Biol. Rev., **15**:202.
80. ———. 1947. Observations on the anatomy of the fossil Australopithecinae, J. Anat., **81**:300.
81. ———. 1950. New palaeontological evidence bearing on the evolution of the Hominoidea, Quart. J. Geol. Soc., **105**:225.
82. ———. 1950. Hominid characters of the australopithecine dentition, J. Roy. Anthrop. Inst., **80**:37.
83. ———. 1952. A note on certain cranial indices of the Sterkfontein skull No. 5, Am. J. Phys. Anthropol., **10**:1.
84. ———. 1954. History of the Primates. 4th ed. London: British Museum (Nat. Hist.).
85. ———. 1953. Growth and body proportions in relation to the systematics of the higher Primates, Proc. Linnean Soc. London, **164**: 140.
86. LE GROS CLARK, W. E., and LEAKEY, L. S. B. 1951. The Miocene Hominoidea of East Africa. ("Fossil mammals of Africa," No. 1.) London: British Museum (Nat. Hist.).
87. LE GROS CLARK, W. E., and THOMAS, D. P. 1951. Associated jaws and limb bones of *Limnopithecus macinnesi.* ("Fossil mammals of Africa," No. 3.) London: British Museum (Nat. Hist.).
88. LEWIS, G. E. 1934. Preliminary notice of new man-like apes from India, Am. J. Sc., **27**:161.
89. MAYR, E. 1942. Systematics and the origin of species. New York: Columbia University Press.
90. ———. 1950. Taxonomic categories in fossil hominids, Cold Spring Harbor Symp. Quant. Biol., **15**:109.
91. McCOWN, T. D., and KEITH, A. 1939. The Stone Age of Mount Carmel. Oxford: Clarendon Press.
92. MORANT, G. M. 1927. Studies of Palaeolithic man. II. A biometric study of Neanderthaloid skulls and their relationships to modern racial types, Ann. Eugenics, **2**:318.
93. ———. 1928. Studies of Palaeolithic man. III. The Rhodesian skull and its relations to Neanderthaloid and modern types, *ibid.*, **3**:337.
94. ———. 1938. The form of the Swanscombe skull, J. Roy. Anthrop. Inst., **68**:67.
95. MOVIUS, H. L. 1944. Early man and Pleistocene stratigraphy in southern and eastern Asia. ("Papers of the Peabody Museum of American Archeology and Ethnology, Harvard University," Vol. **19.**)
96. NAPIER, J. R. 1959. Fossil metacarpals from Swartkrans. Fossil Mammals of Africa, No. 17. London: British Museum (Nat. Hist.).
97. ———. 1962. Fossil hand bones from Olduvai gorge. Nature, **196**: 409.

References

98. NAPIER, J. R. 1964. The evolution of bipedal walking in the hominids, Proc. 2d Internat. European Anatomical Congress.
99. NAPIER, J. R., and WEINER, J. S. 1962. Olduvai gorge and human origins, Antiquity, **36**:41.
100. NOBACK, C. R., and Moss, M. L. 1953. The topology of the human premaxillary bone, Am. J. Phys. Anthropol., **11**:181.
101. OAKLEY, K. P. 1950. New studies on Rhodesian man, J. Roy. Anthrop. Inst., **77**:7.
102. ———. 1951. A definition of man, Sc. News, **20**:69.
103. ———. 1953. Dating fossil human remains. *In:* KROEBER, A. L. (ed.), Anthropology today, p. 43. Chicago: University of Chicago Press.
104. ———. 1954. Dating of the Australopithecinae of Africa, Am. J. Phys. Anthropol., **12**:9.
105. OAKLEY, K. P., and MONTAGU, M. F. A. 1949. A reconsideration of the Galley Hill skeleton, Bull. Brit. Mus. (Nat. Hist.), Geol. Ser., **2**:46.
106. OPPENOORTH, W. F. F. 1932. *Homo (Javanthropus) soloensis:* een Plistoceene mensch von Java, Wetensch. Meded. Dienst Mijnbouw Nederlandsch-Indië, **20**:49.
107. PEARSON, K., and BELL, J. 1919. A study of the long bones of the English skeleton, Part I, Sec. II. ("Drapers Company Research Mem., Biometric Ser.," Vol. XI.)
108. PYCRAFT, W. P., *et al.* 1928. Rhodesian man and associated remains. London: British Museum (Nat. Hist.).
109. REMANE, A. 1922. Beiträge zur Morphologie des Anthropoidengebisses, Arch. f. Naturgesch., **87**:1.
110. ———. 1927. Studien ueber die Phylogenie des menschlichen Eckzahnes, Ztschr. f. Anat. u. Entwicklungsgesch., **82**:391.
111. ———. 1951. Die Zähne des *Meganthropus africanus*, Ztschr. f. Morphol. u. Anthropol., **42**:311.
112. ROBINSON, J. T. 1952. The Australopithecine-bearing deposits of the Sterkfontein area, Ann. Transvaal. Mus., **22**:1.
113. ———. 1952. Some hominid features of the ape-man dentition, J. Dent. A. South Africa, March 15, p. 1.
114. ———. 1953. *Meganthropus,* australopithecines and hominids, Am. J. Phys. Anthropol., **11**:1.
115. ———. 1953. The nature of *Telanthropus,* Nature, **171**:33.
116. ———. 1954. The genera and species of the Australopithecinae, Am. J. Phys. Anthropol., **12**:181.
117. ———. 1955. Further remarks on the relationship between "*Meganthropus*" and *Australopithecus africanus, ibid.,* **13**:429.
118. ———. 1956. The Dentition of the Australopithecinae, Transvaal Mus. Mem., No. 9.

194

119. SCHULTZ, A. H. 1931. Man as a Primate, Scient. Month., **33**:385.
120. ———. 1935. Eruption and decay of the permanent teeth in Primates, Am. J. Phys. Anthropol., **19**:489.
121. ———. 1936. Characters common to higher Primates and characters specific for man, Quart. Rev. Biol., **11**:259, 425.
122. ———. 1950. The anatomy of the gorilla, p. 227. New York: Columbia University Press.
123. ———. 1950. The physical distinctions of man, Proc. Am. Phil. Soc., **94**:428.
124. ———. 1960. Einige beobachtungen und Masse am Skelett von *Oreopithecus*, Zeitschr. Morph. Anthr., **50**:136.
125. ———. 1962. Schadelkapazität mannlicher Gorillas und ihr Hochstwert, Anthr. Anz. **25**:197.
126. SERGI, S. 1943. Craniometria e iconografia del secondo Paleantropo di Saccopastore, Rend. Accad. Italia, **7**:41.
127. ———. 1944. Craniometria e craniografia del primo Paleantropo di Saccopastore. *In:* Estratto delle Ricerche di Morfologia, p. 1. Rome: Istituto di Anthropologia della Università di Roma.
128. SHELLSHEAR, J., and ELLIOT SMITH, G. 1934. A comparative study of the endocranial cast of *Sinanthropus*, Phil. Tr. Roy. Soc., B, **223**:469.
129. SIMONS, E. L. 1961. The Phyletic position of *Ramapithecus*, Postilla, New Haven: Peabody Museum (Yale University), No. 57.
130. ———. 1963. A critical reappraisal of Tertiary Primates. From Evolutionary and Genetic Biology of Primates, Vol. 1. New York: Acad. Press, Inc.
131. ———. 1963. Some fallacies in the study of hominid phylogeny. Science, **141**:879.
132. SIMPSON, G. C. 1945. The principles of classification and a classification of mammals, Bull. Am. Mus. Nat. Hist., Vol. **85**.
133. ———. 1950. The meaning of evolution. London: Oxford University Press.
134. ———. 1950. Some principles of historical biology bearing on human origins, Cold Spring Harbor Symp. Quant. Biol., **15**:55.
135. ———. 1951. Horses. London: Oxford University Press.
136. SINGER, R. 1954. The Saldanha skull from Hopefield, South Africa, Am. J. Phys. Anthropol., **12**:345.
137. SOLECKI, R. S. 1960. Three adult Neanderthal skeletons from Shanidar cave in Northern Iraq, Smithsonian Rep. Publ. No. 4414, 603.
138. STEKELIS, M.; PICARD, L.; SCHULMAN, N.; and HAAS, G. 1960. Villafranchian deposits near Ubeidya in the Central Jordan Valley, Preliminary report. Bull. Res. Council Israel, **9**:175.

References

139. STEWART, T. D. 1960. Form of the pubic bone in Neanderthal Man, Science, **131**:1437.

140. STRAUS, W. L. 1949. The riddle of man's ancestry, Quart. Rev. Biol., **24**:200.

141. SWANSCOMBE COMMITTEE OF THE ROYAL ANTHROPOLOGICAL INSTITUTE. 1938. Report on the Swanscombe skull, J. Roy. Anthrop. Inst., **68**:17.

142. TERRA, M. DE. 1905. Beiträge zu einer Odontographie der Menschenrasse. Inaug. Diss. Zurich: H. Freise.

143. TOBIAS, P. V. 1963. Cranial capacity of *Zinjanthropus* and other australopithecines, Nature, **197**:743.

144. TWIESSELMAN, F. 1961. Le Fémur Néanderthalien de Ford-de-Forêt, Mem. Inst. Roy. de Sc. Nat. de Belgique, **148**:1.

145. VALLOIS, H. V. 1945. L'Homme fossile de Rabat, C.R. Acad. Sc. **211**:669.

146. ———. 1949. The Fontéchevade fossil man, Am. J. Phys. Anthropol., **7**:339.

147. WASHBURN, S. L. 1942. Technique in primatology, Anthrop. Briefs, No. 1, p. 6.

148. ———. 1950. The analysis of Primate evolution, with particular reference to the origin of man, Cold Spring Harbor Symp. Quant. Biol., **15**:67.

149. WASHBURN, S. L., and PATTERSON, B. 1951. Evolutionary importance of the South African man-apes, Nature, **167**:650.

150. WATSON, D. M. S. 1951. Palaeontology and modern biology. New Haven: Yale University Press.

151. WEIDENREICH, F. 1928. Der Schädelfund von Weimar-Ehringsdorf. Jena: Gustav Fischer.

152. ———. 1936. The mandibles of *Sinanthropus pekinensis,* Palaeont. Sinica, Ser. D, Vol. 1.

153. ———. 1937. The dentition of *Sinanthropus pekinensis,* Palaeont. Sinica, Ser. D, Vol. 1.

154. ———. 1939. On the earliest representatives of modern mankind recovered on the soil of East Asia, Pekin Nat. Hist. Bull., **13**:161.

155. ———. 1941. The extremity bones of *Sinanthropus pekinensis,* Palaeont. Sinica, No. 116.

156. ———. 1943. The skull of *Sinanthropus pekinensis, ibid.,* No. 127.

157. ———. 1945. Giant early man from Java and South China, Anthrop. Papers, Am. Mus. Nat. Hist., **40**:1.

158. ———. 1951. Morphology of Solo man, *ibid.,* **43**:205.

159. WEINER, J. S.; OAKLEY, K. P.; and LE GROS CLARK, W. E. 1953. The solution of the Piltdown problem, Bull. Brit. Mus. (Nat. Hist.), Geol. Ser., **2**: No. 3, 141.

160. WEINERT, H. 1936. Der Urmenschenschädel von Steinheim, Ztschr. f. Morphol. u. Anthropol., **35**:463.
161. ———. 1951. Ueber die neuen Vor- und Frühmenschenfunde aus Afrika, Java, China und Frankreich, *ibid.*, **42**:113.
162. WELLS, L. H. 1950. New studies on Rhodesian man, J. Roy. Anthrop. Inst., **77**:11.
163. WOO, JU-KANG. 1963. Ape or Man? From China Reconstructs, **12**:8.
164. YATES, F., and HEALEY, M. J. R. 1951. Statistical methods in anthropology, Nature, **168**:1116.
165. ZAPFE, H. 1960. Die Primatenfunde aus der miozänen Spaltenfüllung von Neudorf, Schweiz. Paleont. Abhandl., **78**:1.
166. ZEUNER, F. E. 1940. The age of Neanderthal man. ("Occasional Papers of the Institute of Archaeology, University of London," No. 3.)
167. ZUCKERMAN, S. 1928. Age-changes in the chimpanzee, with special reference to growth of brain, eruption of teeth, and estimation of age, Proc. Zoöl. Soc., p. 1.

Index

Index